BLACK AND GREEN

Black Insights for the Green Movement

Jamal Ali

Hamilton Books
A member of
The Rowman & Littlefield Publishing Group
Lanham · Boulder · New York · Toronto · Plymouth, UK

Hamilton Books
4501 Forbes Boulevard
Suite 200
Lanham, Maryland 20706
Hamilton Books Acquisitions Department (301) 459-3366

Estover Road
Plymouth PL6 7PY
United Kingdom

Library of Congress Control Number: 2009929776
ISBN-13: 978-0-7618-4721-2 (cloth : alk. paper)
ISBN-10: 0-7618-4721-9 (cloth : alk. paper)
ISBN-13: 978-0-7618-4722-9 (paperback : alk. paper)
ISBN-10: 0-7618-4722-7 (paperback : alk. paper)
eISBN-13: 978-0-7618-4723-6
eISBN-10: 0-7618-4723-5

Cover photograph by Christen James

Author photograph by Robert Levite

For Rosalind, Arshad, and Amirah

Table of Contents

Preface   *vii*

Acknowledgements   *xi*

Introduction: Reuse Is Not New to Black People   *xiii*

Chapter 1: Going Green Starts at Home   *1*

Chapter 2: Rediscovering Your Neighborhood   *11*

Chapter 3: Food and Its Environmental Impact   *17*

Chapter 4: The Electric Car Is Here   *21*

Chapter 5: Invoking Green in Education   *27*

Chapter 6: Cashing In on Green   *33*

Chapter 7: Black Institutions That Should Be Green   *37*

Chapter 8: Bury Me Green   *47*

Chapter 9: The Future of Green   *51*

End Notes   *59*

Resource Guide   *63*

Index   *67*

Preface

Malcolm X once said that when you live in a poor neighborhood, you attend a poor school. When you attend a poor school, you get a poor education. With a poor education, you can only get a poor paying job. With a poor paying job, you can only live in a poor neighborhood—so it's a vicious cycle.

Today, in many inner-city neighborhoods where Black people live, that cycle not only continues, but it has gotten progressively worse. Inner cities are currently plagued with gun violence and murder; high unemployment, particularly among Black men, gang warfare, a nearly 50% average high school dropout rate, health problems, including higher than average obesity levels among children, heart disease, diabetes, asthma and HIV AIDS. Any one of these problems could stifle progress in a community. But when almost all of these problems exist simultaneously and continue to rise, the results are alarming.

Many of these problems are outgrowths of the community itself—that cycle. Where we live and how we live contribute to these factors as much as anything else. What we eat and drink and how we live and interact with others in and outside our community are all related to the environment in which we live. This relates back to that cycle.

There are many reports that suggest living in the city decreases life expectancy by as much as five years. Living in very close proximity, which is the case in many of our neighborhoods, adds to our frustration. The lack of fresh fruits and vegetables in our neighborhoods contributes to poor health. Inner-city schools are overcrowded and underfunded, which usually results in failing test scores, school closings, and children being reshuffled. I could continue to deconstruct each of these problems, but I think you get the picture.

I realize that it is quite a stretch to introduce saving the environment, or "going green" as one possible solution for many of our problems. However, I might as well begin to make my case here and now.

In the summer of 2007, my wife and I began to have discussions on the front porch about the constant information we were reading, hearing, and seeing about going green. We started taking notice of how green initiatives were benefiting communities. We noticed that very little, if any, information focused on the Black community. As I began to delve into various aspects of going green, I became excited about the possibilities in our community. This coupled with the fact that, at that time, I had not heard of any Black person locally or nationally out front on this issue. I knew I was going to be among the first to issue the call to my community to go green.

While it was fairly easy to come up with ideas on *how* to get Black people to embrace the green movement, identifying the reasons *why* we should go green proved to be the bigger challenge.

As I attempted to address this question, I realized that the more common reasons given to get us to help save the environment (global warming, melting ice glaciers in the Arctic and thinning ozone) were not going to mobilize my community—at least not yet. I decided that if I was going to make the case for why Black people should embrace the green movement, I needed to bring it to the local level, in a way that could break the cycle.

If I could make the connection that many of the problems facing our community can be traced to the environment, I just might get the attention of my community. There are many reasons why Black people should embrace the green movement. Here are a few:

- **Reduction in Crime**

    If the Black community mobilized, making sure our neighborhoods were clean, reflecting the fact that somebody cares, then crime would have to drop. If people start walking, biking, cleaning their neighborhoods, and having a say in the types of businesses that come into the community, our streets and blocks would become vital, exude safety and, more importantly, reflect organization.

    This progress has to start with the Black man. If the Black man became concerned about the water he drinks, the air he breathes, the food he eats, the neighborhood he lives in, he would certainly be concerned about the temple within himself. Once he understands that his body, fueled by his mind, is a temple, he will then see the temple in his brother and thus will not want to do harm to another.

- **Job Creation**

    Some experts are already saying that green is and will continue to be an economic engine creating jobs born from new industries and technologies. Contractors will be needed to install tankless water heaters, photovoltaic and solar panels, and retrofit homes and appliances to become more energy efficient. More inspectors will be needed to license buildings as Leadership in Energy and Environmental Design (LEED) certified. New green products will increase competition, which will in turn intensify the marketing of those goods and services. These and many other green jobs are already there for the taking and this is a great opportunity for the Black community to get in on the ground floor.

- **Better Health**

     Most of us who live in the inner city realize that the majority of the food we eat, which should help sustain life, actually slowly takes life away from us. We eat a lot of processed foods, drink a lot of soda, and when we prepare our food, we like it fried, and we like it with salt. The results of these habits are heart disease, high blood pressure, diabetes, obesity, and many other health problems. If we start to reduce our food intake and then start to monitor what we eat, how it is prepared and how it is grown, many of our health problems would improve and possibly disappear.

- **More Money**

     Going green essentially means ascribing to the 3 Rs: Reducing, Reusing and Recycling. Inherent in these principles are money-saving techniques. If we start to consume less—buying less food, driving less, using less water and electricity—we will save money and help save the environment. Reusing as much as we can before recycling will further save money and help save the environment.

Finally, as the call continues to go out to get individuals, groups, cities, towns, and governments to go green, I have joined in that call to the Black community. A community that is talented, diverse, and dynamic. A community that turned the music industry upside down and created the hip-hop revolution. It continues to influence urban fashion and other cultural trends. This group of people, my community, needs to go green, and a big start to achieving this is to make green "cool." If green is perceived as being cool, Black people will be all over it. Green would not just be "green," there would be degrees of green— denoting the depths of green cool, e.g., "2Green," "GreenedUp," "Phat Green." It is time we made green cool, if that is what it takes to get the community on board. In the meantime, I am issuing the call to the Black community to embrace the green movement as it stands right now.

Jamal Ali

Acknowledgements

There are too many people to thank for helping to make this book a reality and, while some will undoubtedly be omitted, I want to acknowledge as many as I can.

First, I want to thank Samantha Kirk and the Editorial Board at University Press of America, the publisher of this book, for believing in my idea.

Thank you to my editors, Christy Parrish and Lisa Weathersby. Christy Parrish did the initial edit of the manuscript, which really put me on the path to completing this book. My friend Lisa Weathersby has lived with this project since its inception. While she did the final edit, she added so much more. Beyond her great editing skills lies an amazing gift of patience, which she demonstrated with me throughout this long journey. I am certain this book would not have been completed without her involvement. Thanks to Susan Maldovan who added so much more to this book beyond her proofreading talents.

Before the editing could be done, however, Dr. Karen A. Chachere, my friend and neighbor, helped me with organization, structure, stylistics, and grammar. Her insights on Black culture helped me tremendously.

Several friends and colleagues reviewed the manuscript and provided invaluable insights and ideas. Thanks to all of you, including Byron Lewis, Robert Levite, Jill Rahman, Melissa Hibbert, Manuel Glaze, Janeen Ebster, Marcia Delaney, Shareef Muhammad and Tommy Diggs.

On a Metra train ride from O'Hare Airport into the city of Chicago, I first met Neal Lurie, director of marketing for the American Solar Energy Association. During our conversation, Neal gave me a report on energy efficiency and renewable energy, from which I was able to use some of the material for this book. In addition, Neal connected me with the office of Van Jones. Mr. Jones's office provided information that allowed me to introduce him in the chapter "Cashing in on Green."

Thanks to Rhea Kaufman of the Environmental Policy Institute for granting me permission to use information from Lester Brown's book, *Plan B 2.0 Rescuing a Planet Under Stress and a Civilization in Trouble*.

Thanks to Mark Lane of Mark Lane Investment Management, Inc., the *Chicago Tribune Magazine*, The Museum of Science and Industry, and *EV World* magazine for granting permission to reprint material that was essential to completing this work.

Thanks to my friend and brother, Munir Muhammad, who for several years encouraged me to write a book.

Finally, I would like to thank my wife and best friend, Rosalind, who first encouraged me to write this book. She read the manuscript countless times and offered many ideas that are present throughout this work. She has always been there to provide that steadfast encouragement.

"In today's world, you can be Black and Navy too."
This is a quote from a U.S. Navy radio commercial that I remember from many years ago as a child in Birmingham, Alabama.

Introduction:
Reuse Is Not New to Black People

When I was growing up in Birmingham, Alabama, my dad would often come home and notice several lights on in rooms that no one was using. This would lead him to proclaim, "Every light is on in the house." Obviously, the electric bill, or "light bill" as he called it, was just one of the expenses he was trying to contain while providing for a wife and seven children.

Years later, after being out on my own, I remain cognizant of the conservation lessons I learned from my dad. Not only do I pay attention to unattended lights, but I also turn off the faucet while brushing my teeth and do not waste energy standing in front of the refrigerator with the door open to assess what is inside. If I have a lapse in paying attention to even one of these rules, I feel guilty. The lessons from my childhood have helped to prepare me for the time at hand.

Saving the environment is a major issue for our lifetime. This "green" movement, as it is often called, is gaining momentum. Part of this momentum was fueled by former Vice President Al Gore's documentary, *An Inconvenient Truth.*

When I was in elementary school, I recall teachers aggressively trying to prepare us for the metric system shift, because America's complete standard of measurement was going to be converted to the metric system. We were drilled on the metric equivalents of such things as pints, gallons, inches, and miles. Today, although we see markers along major highways showing distances in miles followed by the equivalent distance in kilometers, and most of us have purchased a liter of Coca-Cola,™ we still have not fully adopted metric measures into our vernacular and way of life, certainly not to the extent that we were warned about in elementary school.

I don't think the warnings about saving the environment and the need to go green will fade in the way that the "metric shift" did. Although there was no moral imperative for converting to the metric system, there is a moral imperative for going green. In fact, I am certain the push to go green will increase in the coming years, as we continue to see rising energy and fuel prices, and extreme weather that is increasingly unpredictable—deserts flooding, cold weather where it is normally hot and vice versa. Greenhouse gases, melting glaciers, holes in the ozone layer, and rising earth temperatures—the debate will continue regarding the relevance of these factors to our daily lives or whether these factors are even real.

Regardless of which side one stands on in these debates and even if one decides not to take a stand at all, rising energy and fuel prices (real costs that we recognize and live with every day) will continue to be a reality. As a result, inherent in these debates is the need to identify alternative and renewable energy and the need to reduce, reuse, and recycle as much as we can in an effort to save the environment. This is one of the most important issues we will confront in our lifetime.

You may be wondering, "Why should I care?" In a few years, there may come a time when there is not only a gasoline shortage but also a water shortage. I do not simply mean being unable to water our lawns or wash our cars. We could very well see a day when there is not enough clean drinking water to supply cities and towns. Though we might have plenty of money, great jobs, nice clothes, and fine automobiles, we will not be able to enjoy the quality of life to which we have become accustomed. Imagine citizens in an uproar, and cities in crises. This could very well happen.

The call to save the environment, or go green, will be for every person, every household, every school, and every business to do their part. To date, this call to go green has not resonated in the Black community, at least to the extent of generating ongoing discussions and participation. This could be due to a number of reasons:

- **No sense of urgency.** Although we are experiencing climate changes and erratic conditions, we may not see many of the global problems in our lifetime. Why worry now?
- **How does it affect me?** I hear you, but what does it have to do with me personally?
- **Key institutions in the Black community have not embraced going green.** Why should I do it if my minister or my church has not seen the need go green?

- **In the overall scheme of things, going green is not on my radar.**
  Major focus could be on providing for the family, paying bills, making
  sure the children are safe, or simply making do.
- **I've worked hard to get where I am, and I want to live a little.**
  There is no time now to focus on conserving. There is a large segment
  of Black professionals that associate success with the accumulation of
  wealth and material things—the bling, bling. And bling does not go
  with green.

It is unfortunate that the Black community has not embraced the green
movement because we could fuel this movement based on our experience. If
saving the environment is, in part, predicated on reuse, you can't find a people
with better reuse experience than Black people.

When we were first loaded and stacked spoon-fashion in the bowels of
slave ships headed for America, we quickly had to become a "make do" people—to make the most out of what we had. The conditions on the slave ships
were subhuman at best and the food, or what was considered food, was drasti-
cally different from the fresh fruits and vegetables our ancestors were accustomed to eating. And since there was no guarantee that there would be enough
food to go around, the slaves had to learn how to stretch the meager portions.
Many slaves, male and female, actually jumped overboard rather than continue
to endure life on the ships. Only the ablest survived the long journey from Africa to the Caribbean and then to America, where they would live and die as
slaves. When the slaves finally landed on the shores of North America, they
were thoroughly immersed in making do.

On the plantation, our ancestors had to make do with food the slave master
deemed unfit to for his own consumption. They managed to survive on the ears,
brains, feet, tongue, and entrails of animals—the low-end parts of animals. The
phrase "living high on the hog" suggests the good life; but from a literal perspective, it means eating the upper portions of the hog, which were considered
better (i.e., the ham, chops and tenderloins). The slaves were left with the entrails, the very soul of the animal—which many believe is the true origin of the
term soul food.

As we say in the neighborhood, we have always had to "rob Peter to pay
Paul." While other people may have struggled to make ends meet, Black people
settled for getting the ends to point in the same direction. If life handed us lem-
ons, which would have been considered a blessing, we would have made lemon
pound cake, lemon meringue pies, and lemon ice cream. And at the very end of
the supply chain, we would have found time to make a little lemonade for ourselves, as well as a little bit to sell.

As part of our experience in this country, we learned how to get a dollar out
of a dime. We added milk to eggs to make them fluffy to stretch the portion in
order to feed another mouth. It didn't take a lot to live on or since we didn't
have the means to be choosy, we made the best out of what little we had. We

made do. A neck bone and a few peas made a meal with a pan of hot water corn-bread. Everything in the refrigerator at the end of the week was combined into a soup. Aluminum foil was used and reused until it became . . . just foil.

When I was growing up, almost every house in my neighborhood had a garden. We ate fresh vegetables often, and we did not stock the pantry with canned goods. We did not make daily trips to the grocery store to buy bread, milk, sugar, or other items as we do today. Money was tight so we bought in bulk to reduce costs.

This practice was not limited to food either. I remember when we would mend the knees of our jeans with iron-on patches. It was no big deal because everybody did it. Washed clothes were hung out to dry on the clothesline—dryers were not common during those days. Every teenager and adult in the household did not own a car, as is common today. We hitched rides with the person who had a car to go to our jobs or other places, even on dates. The way we lived life back then would be considered basic today. If that's the case, it's time we got back to the basics in an effort to help save the environment.

In this book, you will learn that everyone can and should start going green, and whether you live in a house, an apartment, a trailer, or a tent, we all can make a difference. I will show how going green in many instances saves money but also that going green is always smart and saves energy. Here is the path I take to get Black people focused on going green.

Going Green Starts at Home

While there is nothing Black about installing compact fluorescent light bulbs (CFLs), I make a point that many Black people opt for the budget payment plans for utilities to better manage the rising energy costs. Urging Black people to convert to CFLs, however, is one way we can take action to reduce energy costs. I show how, in every room, there are ways to help save the environment. I shed light on the harmful chemicals used for cleaning and highlight the many clothes we buy and wear and how those clothes affect the environment. Surprisingly, even the bed we sleep on has environmental implications.

Rediscovering Your Neighborhood

Our communities would look significantly better if we initiated green projects. I even suggest that crime, which is a major issue in most Black communities, would decrease if the neighborhood got energized and got serious about going green.

Food and Its Environmental Impact

Many Black communities are trapped in "food deserts." This term refers to neighborhoods that do not have quality grocery stores in the immediate vicinity where its residents live. In order to get fresh fruit and vegetables, in many in-stances residents have to travel great distances. It is no wonder that many Black people suffer from high blood pressure, heart disease, diabetes, and other problems related to diet.

I explain how food plays a part in saving the environment—whether considering organic or healthier food offerings to doing our shopping locally, what we eat and how it gets to our tables have an environmental impact.

The Electric Car Is Here

Despite living in a time where fuel prices will continue to rise, I don't see many Black people driving hybrids. I explain why considering a hybrid vehicle makes sense, and I show why adding a little more style to the eco-friendly vehicles would further attract Black consumers. I explore why there is a push to improve on the hybrid with a fully electric automobile.

Invoking Green in Education

In addition to making green a part of our local schools' curricula, this chapter shows how some colleges and universities are going green and how Historically Black Colleges and Universities (HBCUs) can do the same. Imagine an HBCU-Black Farmer Initiative, whereby a partnership could be formed to save the shrinking Black farms. I illustrate how this can be done.

Cashing In on Green

Going green doesn't just mean conserving energy; it can also mean investing in companies that balance profit-generating strategies with efforts to reduce their carbon footprint. I explain why Socially Responsible Investments (SRIs) are becoming more popular.

Black Institutions That Should Be Green

This section features some predominantly Black cities that should be focusing on green. In addition, an event such as the ever-popular family reunion is a great opportunity to invoke green initiatives. And yes, I point out that, of all our institutions, the Black church should be the focal point for saving the environment.

Bury Me Green

This chapter illustrates that even in death, we can make sure that our efforts to go green continue by eliminating many of the traditional funeral procedures and costs, opting for a simple yet meaningful burial. I point out that we sometimes make emotional decisions about coffins and clothing and other things that go into the ground and are never being seen again. Burying green offers an eco-friendly approach to the standard burial.

The Future of Green

To get a peek at the future of green, I traveled to Greensburg, Kansas. The town was literally wiped out by a tornado on May 4, 2007, and city officials decided to rebuild the entire city green. While very few Black people live in Greensburg, the idea can be replicated in any city in the country.

Chapter 1
Going Green Starts at Home

Where we live—our house, apartment, or mobile home—represents the largest component of our household budget, approximately 30%.[1] The home is where we spend most of our time, where we eat, relax, and sleep—where we live. Among the things we do to make a place livable is to clean it. Some of us clean more than others. I am sure each of us has friends or relatives who clean too often, and others who clean the house only when there is a potential health risk. Fortunately, most of us are in the category where we view house cleaning as part of an everyday routine. We use dishes and we wash them afterwards. We make our beds daily or regularly, we hang up our clothes, we make sure our kitchen floors are clean, and we definitely make sure the bathroom is clean.

Green Cleaning

As Black people, we like to see the lather and to smell cleaning products to know they are working—the stronger the smell, we tend to think, the better the cleaning properties. But, this cannot be good for us. Just as we read food labels, we should read labels on cleaning products. Many of the popular products we use are laced with chemicals that are harmful to the environment and harmful to us. We lock these products away from our children because the chemicals they contain can be dangerous. Most people don't know that manufacturers of cleaning products are not required to list ingredients on labels.[2] Yet we continue to buy these products. There are some green alternatives that are just as effective. Green cleaning is not only environmentally safe, but it is also much more cost-effective when you compare the costs of natural products, such as vinegar and baking soda, to the popular name brands.

I grew up hearing a commercial for a detergent called Fab, which touted a new ingredient called borax. I always wondered what borax was. Borax, or sodium borate, is a naturally occurring alkaline mineral.[3] It is perhaps most widely used as a detergent booster, but it can be used for general household cleaning. Just as with baking soda, add white vinegar to borax and you can clean the toilet, tub, or kitchen counter.

Going green with household cleaning is not only smart, economical, and environmentally safe, but green cleaning is actually a healthier choice when you consider breathing in the fumes from chemical-laced products.

In the Kitchen

When it comes to going green, the kitchen is a good place to start. From the food we eat to the appliances we use to cook the food to the cleansers we use to clean the kitchen, all present opportunities to save the environment. Start by noticing what you throw away and look to reuse and recycle as much as you can. Use a box, a separate trash can, or any type of container to collect plastic, glass, aluminum cans, and other recyclables.

In the sink, add an aerator to the faucet to improve water efficiency. These cost about $4. The flow will feel stronger, but it actually contains less water and more air. Conventional faucets use five to fifteen gallons a minute; aerated faucets reduce use to three gallons per minute—this saves money over the long term.[4]

Most of us know by now that plastic water bottles require an enormous amount of energy to produce and transport to your local grocery store. Another major problem with plastic bottles is that they are usually found in litter in our streets, yards, and playgrounds. They have become part of floating plastic islands that trap and kill fish and other species. Many people who are concerned about the environment have begun reusing water bottles. This presents a new problem. Many of these water bottles are made from a hard plastic called polyethylene terephthalate (PET). The material is safe for single use and is not intended for constant reuse. Even reusable water bottles should be under scrutiny along with all the plastic food containers in your home.[5] Most plastic containers will have the "recycle" symbol underneath the container which are three arrows in the shape of a triangle. Inside the triangle is a number ranging from 1-7. Numbers 1, 2, 4 and 5 are considered safe to reuse while numbers 3, 6 and 7 should be avoided.[6]

We can eliminate the need to buy bottled water simply by boiling tap water in stainless steel pots or pans. This water can be poured into glass bottles or stainless steel containers to take to work or to put into your child's lunch. To be more efficient, store large quantities of water in pitchers and drink from a reusable glass or cup.

To save energy when cooking, turn off the oven and stove near the end of the cooking process. The heat generated from the oven, skillet, pot, or pan will allow the cooking process to continue.[7]

Look for appliances with the Energy Star® label. Energy Star is a program that was first developed in 1992 by the U.S. Environmental Protection Agency

(EPA) as a method to identify and promote products that are energy efficient. Products carrying this label provide a way for businesses and consumers to save money while at the same time protecting the environment. Since its onset, the government has partnered with other industry members to promote and expand the scope of the Energy Star program to include not only major appliances but also new homes and buildings. A major appliance that sports the Energy Star® label is not necessarily a better product than a comparable model, but in order to receive the Energy Star rating, it must meet very strict energy efficiency guidelines.[8]

There have also been many major advances in technology, leading to such energy savers as liquid crystal display (LCD) lighting and stand-by product features. Research and development continues as manufacturers strive to deliver low-cost energy products.

Be environmentally conscious when using your appliances. For example, only run the dishwasher when you have a full load of dishes.[9] Scrape food off plates, utensils, and cookware instead of using water to rinse them.[10] Whether using a dishwasher or washing dishes manually, use low-phosphate or phosphate-free soaps and dishwashing liquids. Many popular brands, now widely available, have low phosphate levels. Increased phosphorus concentrations cause excessive algae growth in our waterways. Though algae is the basis of life for many ecosystems, an overabundance causes lower levels of dissolved oxygen in the waters, which in turn disrupts ecosystems and causes fish kills. Algae blooms also result in decreased aesthetic and recreational values.[11]

Use power strips for appliances like toasters and can openers to save energy by turning off the switch when you are not using them. Use brown coffee filters made from recycled paper and consider buying a reusable coffee filter. And while you're at it, save used coffee grounds for fertilizer or add them to yard waste and other kitchen waste, such as fruit peelings, wilted lettuce, and tea bags, to make compost, a nutrient-rich soil product which I discuss later in this chapter.

In the Bathroom

In the bathroom we have many opportunities to conserve water. One suggestion is to take showers instead of baths, as showers use less water. There are water-efficient showerheads that reduce water usage even further. Again, using less water lowers your water bill. These devices are sometimes supplied free of charge by your local energy company.

As multi-taskers, we tend to have the shower running while we're doing other things. Be cognizant of the energy you are using so you don't waste water and don't linger in the shower. Shortening your shower by two minutes will save $2.46/week in heating and water costs. Those two minutes will save five gallons of water.[12]

Most people do not know that congress regulates the amount of water held by new toilets.[13] If you have an older model, consider replacing it with an energy-efficient model. Older toilets hold much more water than the new models. There are models that even have dual flush capability, whereby if there is less to flush, there is an option that uses less water and vice versa.

Try replacing your current soap with an environmentally friendly alternative. The Go Green directory is a great source for eco-friendly products. Also, save those tiny pieces of used soap, toss them into a dispenser or cup, and add a little water to make a hand cleanser. This saves money by eliminating the need to buy extra hand cleanser. Remember to always try to get another use out of everything. If more of us would start doing this, we will be well on our way to saving the environment, and we can save money while doing it.

In the Bedroom–Keep Your Mind on Green ☺

Since most of us spend a third of our lives sleeping, we should now make an effort to go green throughout the bedroom. In bidding our children and spouses a good night sleep, why not make sure they sleep comfortably in an eco-friendly way. Here are some ways that you can sleep tight and help save the environment too.

Start with the bed. Most of us concern ourselves with the softness or firmness of the mattress and that's about it. We should be more concerned about what is inside the mattress. Just as the plain cotton used for clothing is laden with pesticides, the cotton used in mattresses contains the same pesticides.[14] You can see where I'm going with this; an organic cotton mattress is an environmentally safe alternative to the traditional mattress. There are also pillows made from recycled polyester and other safe, natural materials that can replace your current model that you've probably had for years. A new, eco-friendly pillow might be just the thing to add to a good night's sleep.

We spend a lot of money on bed linens. We should try to replace the standard fabrics like cotton, flannel, ultra-fine silk and satin with eco-friendly fabrics such as bamboo and organic cotton. In addition to the fine bed linens, furniture, carpets, and curtains all have "green" options.

Here is something to ponder. Have you ever stayed at a hotel where the bed linens and towels were a color other than white? Not hardly; yet we purchase every color of linens and towels in the rainbow. Using all-white linens and towels will save on time needed to sort the various colors for separate laundry loads. This will also help reduce your exposure to the dyes and chemicals needed to make colorful bed linens. As for washing these whites, people tend to believe that the best way to make sure white laundry loads are clean is to wash them in extremely hot water. Hot water uses more energy and should be used only when items are heavily soiled. Otherwise, your clothes will be just as clean when washed in cold water. There are now cold water detergents on the market. Your clothes will last longer and stay brighter when washed in cold water.

When you wash linens and everything else, use only the recommended amount of detergent. I once attended a focus group where to my surprise, and to the surprise of many of the ladies in the group, Black women tend to overdose on the amount of detergent needed for cleaning. We are not satisfied until we see suds bubbling out of the top of the machine—then and only then do we feel the clothes are getting clean. However, most detergents on the market today can clean large loads with small amounts of detergent.

In the Closet—Too Many Clothes

Whoa! I don't mean for our people, especially the ladies, to start wearing fewer clothes. I'm asking the question, "Do we need to own so many pieces of clothing?" We tend to go out and buy clothes for each new season. We wear dresses and suits once and drive to the cleaners to get them dry cleaned only to repeat this process over and over again. As Black people, we place a lot of emphasis on style. We will skip going to church if we feel the congregation has seen us wear a particular outfit recently. There are a number of ways we can go green with clothing.

When we must purchase clothes, look for fabrics that are environmentally friendly, e.g., *organic* cotton, wool, linen, and hemp. Always look for high-quality garments that outlast the ever-appearing fads. Whenever possible, try repairing instead of replacing garments. It is usually much cheaper and requires fewer resources to repair a garment than to purchase a new item.

An even better idea is to consider buying secondhand or gently used clothes for your next purchase. Water is needed to grow cotton and it requires energy to operate factories where clothes are mass-produced. Using clothes already in the supply chain saves these resources. There are plenty of secondhand stores that provide everything from the basics to upscale clothing. In fact, if some of your well-dressed friends would come clean, you might be surprised to know their wardrobe includes secondhand items. Stores like "Bag, Borrow or Steal", allows customers to rent designer purses, such as Louis Vuitton, without paying the hefty purchase price. Whether upscale or not, we need to go green by purchasing more environmentally friendly and secondhand clothes.

Try to get more than one wearing out of some of your garments, such as slacks, shirts, blouses, skirts, dresses, and suits. Unless heavily soiled, these garments should allow for at least one additional wearing. Though this might seem like a small action, it can make a big difference if more people would do it.

Throughout the House—Lighten Up

There are many Black people, particularly those on fixed incomes, who sign up for budget billing plans with their local utilities to help ease the high energy costs during the peak seasons of winter and summer. As energy costs continue to rise, we need to do our part to help control them. When Commonwealth Edison, a supplier of electricity in Chicago, was considering a rate increase after having rates frozen for ten years, CEO Frank Clark reminded customers that they could cut their electric bill costs by adding compact fluorescent light bulbs (CFLs) in high-use areas throughout the home.[15] Some reports have shown that CFLs save about $30 or more in electricity costs over each bulb's lifetime.[16] As I mentioned earlier, turn off unused lights. Think about the energy being wasted the next time you see lights on during daylight hours when the sun is shining through the window. This is a gross waste of energy. Use natural light instead of electricity wherever you can.

Continue to look for other ways to reduce energy costs. The companies that supply our energy are a good resource for information. Visit the Websites of your local utilities for energy-saving tips—here are a few from Peoples Gas in Chicago:

No-cost Tips for Saving Energy and Money

Contrary to popular opinion, you sometimes get more than you pay for. The following energy-saving tips won't cost you a penny—but they can save you bucks on your energy bills.

- Keep your home at seventy-eight degrees in the summer, or at the warmest temperature that is comfortable for you.
- When leaving home for more than four hours, raise the thermostat five to ten degrees in summer and lower it five to ten degrees in winter. Do the same at night before going to bed.
- Close south, east, and west-facing curtains during the day to keep out solar heat during the summer.
- Clean the coils at the back of your refrigerator twice a year.
- Only heat and cool rooms you use; close vents and doors to rooms that are not being used.
- Keep windows closed and shades down when air conditioning is on.
- Check and clean air conditioning filters monthly and replace as needed.
- Unplug electric chargers, televisions, and audio/video equipment when not in use (or plug them into a power strip you can turn off and on). These devices use electricity even when they are not in use.
- Turn off your computer or put it in sleep mode when it is not being used.
- Run energy-intensive appliances, such as the dishwasher and clothes washer at night. The heat produced by these appliances will not need to be offset by your air conditioner during the day.
- Keep lamps and televisions away from the thermostat. The heat they generate will cause your air conditioner to work harder.
- If you're running an old refrigerator in your basement that isn't being used, unplug it. Old refrigerators can use three times the electricity of modern ones.[17]

Commonwealth Edison now offers a program where customers can sign up for alerts to inform them when rates are at their lowest. Ideally a customer would use those appliances that require the most energy, e.g., the furnace, air conditioner, washer and dryer, etc., during this time. I read where one customer lowered his utility costs by approximately 25% compared to the previous year by implementing this program.[18]

In the Yard

Say goodbye to pesticides. Remember, what you put into your yard, or in the ground, will eventually end up in our lakes and rivers. We use all sorts of pesticides on our lawns and in our gardens. Pesticides are intended to kill living organisms. These pesticides spread via wind, air, or runoff, and ultimately make their way into our waterways where they have a devastating impact on plants and fish. Runoff water in most cities is not treated, so let's be careful not to throw trash and other debris into the streets and gutters.[19] Think about rainwater for a moment. Wouldn't this free water be a good resource to capture for reuse to wash the car and water the plants or lawn? This can actually be done. One of the most basic ways is to capture the water in buckets or any type of container. There are also special containers on the market that have screens to trap leaves and debris so that only rainwater flows into the container. For homeowners, consider installing gutters that collect rainwater. As you will see in Chapter 9, "The Future of Green," homes are already being equipped to reuse rainwater for flushing the toilet. Remember—reduce, reuse, recycle!

Convert Yard Waste into Nutrient-Rich Compost

Save yard waste, such as grass clippings, weeds, and other plants that are normally bagged and, in most cases, sent to a landfill. Instead of setting this yard waste out for garbage pickup, start converting this material into nutrient-rich compost. The compost can then be spread back into the soil to help it retain water, which could help improve the efficiency of water usage and help prevent droughts.

What Is Composting?

Composting is nature's way of turning organic waste into a nutrient-rich soil product. Composting works best with adequate water, air, and organic material combined with a good nitrogen-to-carbon ratio. Most experts recommend an 80/20 ratio, with 80% from green matter (e.g., grass clippings, plants, etc.), and 20% from fruit peelings, bread, leaves, pine straw, etc.[20]

Start by compiling the waste matter into a bin, large or small depending on the space you have. Allow air to flow into the container and keep the composting material moist. The compost will generate heat if there is a good ratio of carbon to nitrogen while it cures. Subtle, emanating warmth means that worms, fungi, and bacteria are working hard. When the majority of decomposition has taken place and the compost is ready to be spread on a garden or lawn, the compost will feel cool.[21]

About one-third of your household garbage can be used in compost. Fruit peelings, vegetables, coffee grounds and filters, tea bags, and even some cardboard can be composted. Do not include meat, bones, fish, or dairy products. For outside the house, include leaves, plants, stems, dry grass, and dirt.

While You Are In the Yard—Plant a Tree

Planting trees around the house will eventually provide shade to help reduce temperatures and make the inside of the house cooler. Trees filter the air and water by absorbing carbon monoxide. Trees also hold the soil in place and can help beautify a yard or neighborhood.

Meet Wangari Maathai

A native of Kenya, Wangari Maathai was the first woman in East and Central Africa to earn a doctorate degree. She was active in the National Council of Women of Kenya in 1976-87 and was its chairperson from 1981-87. In 1976, while she was serving the National Council of Women, Professor Maathai introduced the idea of community-based tree planting. She continued to develop this idea into a broad-based grassroots organization whose main focus is poverty reduction and environmental conservation through tree planting. With the organization that became known as the Green Belt Movement, Professor Maathai has assisted women in planting more than 40 million trees on community lands including farms, schools, and church compounds.

In 1986 the Green Belt Movement (GBM) established a Pan-African Green Belt Network that has exposed many leaders of other African countries to its unique approach. Some of these individuals have established similar tree planting initiatives in their own countries using the methods taught to improve their efforts. Countries that have successfully launched such initiatives in Africa include Tanzania, Uganda, Malawi, Lesotho, Ethiopia, Zimbabwe, and others.

In September 1998, Professor Maathai became co-chair of the Jubilee 2000 Africa Campaign, which seeks debt cancellation for African countries. Her campaign against land grabbing and rapacious allocation of forest lands has gained international attention in recent years.

Professor Maathai is internationally recognized for her persistent struggle for democracy, human rights and environmental conservation. She has addressed the UN on several occasions and spoke on behalf of women at special sessions of the General Assembly during the five-year review of the Earth Summit. She served on the commission for Global Governance and the Commission on the Future. She and the Green Belt Movement have received numerous awards, most notably the 2004 Nobel Peace Prize.[22]

As we begin to take steps to help save the environment, beginning first in our own homes, the next step is to organize and move beyond our homes to our neighborhoods in a collective effort, as we will see in the next chapter.

Chapter 2
Rediscovering Your Neighborhood

There are a number of common problems that exist in Black neighborhoods from city to city. Among these are a glut of liquor stores, beauty supply shops, aggressive billboard advertising of liquor and cigarettes, vacant lots, railroad tracks running right through the heart of town and, of course, drugs and crime. If we look hard enough, dump sites and hazardous waste facilities can usually be found in or near Black neighborhoods. In addition to the liquor stores and beauty shops, other businesses such as payday loan shops, pawnshops, and fingernail huts vie for the loyal Black consumer. These factors, over time, wreak havoc on our communities.

The Problem with Vacant Lots
Black neighborhoods tend to have more vacant lots than other neighborhoods. Vacant lots drive down property values and are an invitation to crime, as young Black men tend to use them as gathering places. Our children pass these lots, some with abandoned buildings, every day as they walk to and from school. The owners of the buildings, many of them once beautiful, let them fall into disrepair while continuing to collect rent from tenants until the buildings outlived their usefulness. Then the owners simply stopped paying the taxes on these buildings and let them deteriorate, until they were either torn down or remained as abandoned eyesores. This is a typical situation in many Black neighborhoods.

Wouldn't it be great if these abandoned buildings and vacant lots could be made green by converting them into organic community gardens? The debris-filled lots can be turned into organic vegetable or flower gardens to brighten up a block or corner and make a street look like someone cares. I first learned about community gardens from my wife. Among her memories from childhood is her family's annual summer drive from Detroit to Omaha to visit her grandmother.

She recalls the children's excited anticipation of going grocery shopping as their grandmother called out the ingredients she needed to finish preparing a meal. The excitement, though, was often short-lived as her grandmother would gather a few sacks and make her way not to the grocery store, but to her backyard garden. When her own garden didn't have what she needed, she relied on the community garden down the alley—created and maintained in a vacant lot by neighbors.[1]

The American Community Garden Association's Website is a great resource for information about community gardening. This is their mission statement: "The Association recognizes that community gardening improves people's quality of life by providing a catalyst for neighborhood and community development, stimulating social interaction, encouraging self-reliance, beautifying neighborhoods, producing nutritious food, reducing family food budgets, conserving resources, and creating opportunities for recreation, exercise, therapy, and education."[2] It is clear that a community garden can help to improve Black neighborhoods.

The following steps are adapted from the American Community Garden Association's guidelines for launching a successful community garden in your neighborhood.

1. Organize a Meeting of Interested People

Determine whether a garden is really needed and wanted, what kind it should be (vegetable, flower, both, organic), who will be involved, and who benefits. Invite neighbors, tenants, community organizations, gardening and horticultural societies, and building superintendents (if it involves an apartment building). In other words, invite anyone who is likely to be interested.

2. Form a Planning Committee

This group can be comprised of people who feel committed to the creation of the garden and have the time to devote to it, at least at this initial stage. Choose well-organized people as garden coordinators. Form committees to tackle specific tasks: funding and partnerships, youth activities, construction, and communication.

3. Identify All Your Resources

Do a community asset assessment. What skills and resources already exist in the community that can aid in the garden's creation? Contact local municipal planners about possible sites, as well as horticultural societies and other local sources of information and assistance. Look within your community for people with experience in landscaping and gardening.

4. Approach a Sponsor

Some gardens are able to be "self-supported" through membership dues, but for many, a sponsor is essential for donations of tools, seeds, or money. Churches, schools, private businesses, and parks and recreation departments are all possible supporters. One garden raised money by selling square inches of the garden for $5 each to hundreds of individual sponsors.

5. Choose a Site

Consider the amount of daily sunshine you will need (vegetables need at least six hours a day) and the availability of water. Test the soil for possible pollutants. Find out who owns the land. Can the gardeners get a lease agreement for at least three years? Is public liability insurance needed?

6. Prepare and Develop the Site

In most cases, the land will need considerable preparation for planting. Organize volunteer work crews to clean it, gather materials, and decide on the design and plot arrangement.

7. Organize the Garden

Members must decide how many plots are available and how they will be assigned. Allow space for storing tools and making compost, and don't forget to make pathways between plots. Plant flowers or shrubs around the garden edge to promote goodwill with non-gardening neighbors, passersby, and municipal authorities.

8. Plan for Children

Consider creating a special garden just for children—including them is essential. Children are not as interested in the size of the harvest as they are in the process of gardening. A separate area set aside for them allows them to explore the garden at their own speed.

9. Determine Rules and Put Them in Writing

The gardeners themselves devise the best ground rules. We are more willing to comply with rules that we have had a hand in creating. Ground rules help gardeners to know what is expected of them. Think of it as a code of behavior. Some examples of issues that are best dealt with by agreed upon rules are: How will the dues money be used? How are plots assigned? Will gardeners share tools, meet regularly, handle basic maintenance?

10. Help Members Keep in Touch with Each Other

Good communication ensures a strong community garden with active participation by all. Some ways to do this are: form a telephone tree, create an email list, install a rainproof bulletin board in the garden, and have regular celebrations. Community gardens are all about creating and strengthening communities.[3]

A vacant lot cleanup project has the potential to bring an entire community together. Through the success of one block, other blocks and neighborhoods can be motivated and mobilized to do the same. Again, the vacant lot problem is widespread in our neighborhoods.

Just as we can get organized to plant community gardens, we can continue to organize to address other issues throughout our community. Crime is rampant in our neighborhoods due in part to a lack of organization. A clean yard, street, block, or neighborhood suggests organization, safety, and control. Conversely, when trash remains on the streets, in the gutters, and on the lawns, it is tantamount to advertising that we are not conscious of our surroundings.

If Black men really got involved in cleaning up our communities, the rate of crime would drop. The neighborhoods would be clean and organized—showing energy and vitality. With positive activity being the norm block by block, neighborhood by neighborhood, those individuals who focus on crime will be forced to move elsewhere.

Meet Majora Carter

> *One of the leading figures on African American environmental concerns is Majora Carter. She is the founder of Sustainable South Bronx (SSB), a non-profit environmental justice organization in New York City's South Bronx neighborhood. She is focused on environmental justice and the need for sustainable communities, especially in the nation's poorest neighborhoods.*
>
> *Majora draws a direct connection between ecological, economic and social degradation, hence her motto: "Green the ghetto!" Her organization spearheaded the creation of Hunts Point Riverside Park, the first open-waterfront park in the South Bronx in sixty years. Then she scored $1.25 million in federal funds for greenways along the South Bronx waterfront, bringing the neighborhood open spaces, pedestrian and bike paths, and space for mixed-use economic development. Majora was awarded a 2005 MacArthur "Genius" Grant and now serves as the executive director of Sustainable South Bronx.[4]*

Get Out in Force

Organize a few neighbors to collectively go out to pick up trash together. This will demonstrate that your community is committed to making a difference. In many of our neighborhoods, people have become fed up with the loud music, loitering, and working on cars in the streets. Often, the only action taken is to erect a greeting on the corner that typically might read, "Welcome to Elm Street. NO LOUD MUSIC, WORKING ON CARS, THROWING TRASH."

We have to do more. Getting out in a show of force to clean up the community alerts everybody that your block or your neighborhood means business. This also sends a message to the local businesses to clean up their act, literally. Our communities tend to have businesses owned by people who live outside of the neighborhood. In many cases, these business owners are not concerned about how our communities look or what shape they are in as long as we keep spending. After all, once they have collected your money for the goods and services provided, that money goes to better *their* neighborhoods. When you organize, your collective voice is heard on how these businesses are run and the type of products and services you not only desire but also require. Your collective voice should be heard by local and state government officials. Remember, you can vote with your wallet as well as with the ballot.

Start a Neighborhood Walking Club

It's much easier to get someone to go walking with you than jogging. At your next block club meeting, plan a date to start walking as a group. By getting neighbors to walk together, you can not only improve your health and well-being, you can collectively assess your neighborhood on an ongoing basis and discuss solutions. In many Black neighborhoods, the issues will be the same: litter, vacant lots, abandoned buildings, and crime.

A Green Solution to the Homeless Problem

One day in Chicago, I engaged in a conversation with a man who appeared to be a city worker on cleaning detail. I was intrigued since he was cleaning up my neighborhood. He told me he had been hired by an organization that helped ex-convicts gain meaningful employment. I once suggested such an idea to a local elected official as a way for high school students to share the responsibility of cleaning up their neighborhoods and to make some money in the process. The idea never was implemented nor was it well received.

Today, I cannot go into stores in my neighborhood without being approached by someone asking if I can spare some change to help the homeless. Here is my recommendation to help remedy the homeless problem. Provide jobs for the homeless by expanding programs such as the one I mentioned earlier. Recruit homeless people to not only clean neighborhoods but also to work at recycling facilities separating recyclable materials. More than just a source for some spare change, this would provide the homeless with a steady source of income. Hopefully, this would get them off the streets and into homes.

Chapter 3
Food and Its Environmental Impact

Several health-related problems in the Black community stem from poor diets. Cardiovascular disease (CVD) ranks as the number one killer of Blacks. More than four in every ten Black adults have CVD, which includes stroke, high blood pressure, congestive heart failure, congenital heart defects, hardening of the arteries, and other diseases of the circulatory system. The rate of high blood pressure among Black Americans in the United States is one of the highest in the world.[1]

Studies have shown that among the barriers to eating better, Blacks cite the lack of readily available fresh fruits and vegetables.[2] Our local neighborhood grocery stores certainly don't offer quality meats and abundant supplies of fresh fruits and vegetables. I'm not sure if many of these establishments even qualify as grocery stores. They tend to focus more on peddling beer, wine, liquor, cigarettes, and lottery tickets to Black people than on the fresh meats they advertise on the posters in the windows.

"Food deserts," areas in the inner city lacking grocery stores that sell quality fruits and vegetables, are becoming the norm.[3] Once we begin to focus more on what we eat, we will demand more quality foods. There are ways we can go green, even with the foods we eat.

Give Organic Food a Try

Organic foods continue to gain in popularity as more people become concerned about the food they eat. Organic farmers operate within strict governmental guidelines growing chemical- and pesticide-free fruit, vegetables, and grains, as well as raising livestock that is fed organically-grown grass or feed and not given growth hormones or antibioics.[4]

It might be too costly for consumers to go completely organic all at once, so start by substituting one or two items you regularly buy with an organic alternative. Add more organic items at your own pace and before long, most of your food may be organic. If parents decide not to eat organic, at least consider organic food for your children and definitely for babies. When babies are ready for solid foods, pediatricians recommend introducing one new food at a time to detect any food allergies. Organic baby food is free of all harmful chemicals and it provides another level of protection against allergies.[5] Introducing children to organic foods early may help ensure healthy eating habits throughout their lives.

Think "Environment" When Making Food Choices

In considering the amount of resources needed to produce the food we eat, think for a moment about meat. It requires a huge amount of grain (for feed), fertilizer (for the grain), and water to raise animals for food. It takes almost a hundred times more water to produce one kilogram of animal protein than to produce the same amount of vegetable protein. Livestock also release the greenhouse gas methane as they digest. The meat-centered American diet does not just challenge our arteries, but also our budgets as meat is expensive. If meat is a part of your diet, consider serving smaller portions (two to four ounces per person) with larger servings of produce and whole grains. Another good option may be to eliminate eating meat one day out of each week.[6]

Reports have shown for many years that the growth hormones and antibiotics used in animals raised for food are having adverse effects on our bodies. Young girls are developing breasts and starting their menstrual cycles at much earlier ages. Other studies suggest that penicillin is no longer effective in many people as a result of the antibiotics in the meats they eat.

The average American household throws away approximately 14% of its food purchases, either because the food spoils or we cook too much then toss the leftovers. Before you go grocery shopping, check your refrigerator and shelves to see what you already have, shifting older items to the front. Then make a weekly menu before shopping, so you know exactly how much you need—and don't forget to include leftovers in your meal list. Plan on eating perishable vegetables first; keep fruit in sight so it won't be forgotten.[7]

Eliminate food waste and you'll save landfill space, energy, water, money, and other resources. Add to that the environmental costs associated with growing fruits, vegetables, and grains. If all Americans reduced food waste by 10%, we would prevent millions of pounds of pesticides from being applied to an area roughly the size of New Jersey.[8]

Meet Johari Cole-Kweli

Johari was recently featured in a Chicago Tribune Magazine *cover story about the amazing farming community located in Pembroke, Illinois. She gave up modeling to find that the grass was truly greener in Pembroke. As she stated in the article, "People are surprised to hear about an organic farming community in Pembroke. We have to educate them that Black people were the original organic farmers."*

The farmers describe themselves not as environmentalists, but as caretakers of Mother Earth. They are also preservationists, trying to maintain the history and health of African Americans, whose well-being is under siege, Johari says. She cites some of the dangers: obesity, diabetes, high blood pressure, and heart disease. Food can be a cause and a cure, she says. Many poor people live in "food deserts," barren of decent grocery stores or options.

The farmers also hope to do well by doing good—to use green to make green. In Illinois, the organic-food market has annual sales of $500 million—nearly $17 billion nationwide—and the small farmers of Pembroke are getting in on the action. They sell their pesticide-free produce at farmers' markets in Chicago, Kankakee, and Momence. Last summer, about eight of the farmers pooled their resources and crops from their five-, ten-, and fifteen-acre farms to sell thousands of pounds of fruits and vegetables to a food program for low-income women and children run by Catholic Charities in Chicago.[9]

Try Eating In Sometimes

Green Guide magazine priced a basic chicken meal plus a drink at a popular restaurant chain in the Midwest and compared it with the cost of the ingredients at a nearby grocery store. The cost for four people for the take-out dinner was $45.96. The cost for the ingredients to prepare the meal at home was $20.25, for a savings of $25.71.

The real savings came from packaging and transportation. The paper cups, plastic foam, and takeout containers all require energy and resources to produce, and after a single use, they become part of landfills and waste streams. You also save on the cost of fuel to drive to and from the restaurant.[10]

Farm-Raised Fish Is Better for You, Right?

You may believe that farm-raised fish has been grown under close scrutiny and that it is healthier than the alternatives. The truth is that farm raised does not mean that it is free from hormones and antibiotics. Farmed-raised fish are usually kept in containers where they swim among obviously high concentrations of fish feces and are given antibiotics to prevent disease.[11]

Reward fisheries that go green. These organizations work to protect our rivers, lakes, and oceans. Whenever you can, buy fish that contains the Marine Stewardship Council's seal. This blue oval on the label means that you are supporting fisheries that help to maintain ecosystems by not over fishing and supporting local, national, and international fishing laws.[12]

Shop 'til You Drop Locally

Support your own community. Stop driving long distances to go shopping. Save the gas—save the environment. If you reduce your driving you will put fewer emissions into the atmosphere. Forty-six percent of Black people only sometimes make shopping lists before going to the grocery store, when we do find one that meets our needs.[13] This causes us to drive back and forth every week to pick up items we forgot to purchase—consuming more gas and thus emitting more carbon dioxide into the atmosphere.

Just as we have to travel to the grocery store to purchase food, food and other products have to be transported to the grocery stores. Food miles refer to the distance food travels from the farm to your home. The food miles for items you buy in the grocery store tend to be twenty-seven times higher than the food miles for goods bought from local sources. In the United States, the produce in the average grocery store travels nearly 1,500 miles from the farm where it was grown to your refrigerator.[14] About 40% of the fruit consumed in the U.S. is produced overseas. Although broccoli is likely to be grown within twenty miles of the average American's home, the broccoli we buy at the supermarket travels an average of 1,800 miles. The transportation cost for this produce is passed on to the consumer.[15]

Be more selective when you shop, and at every opportunity buy food that is produced on local farms. Talk to the manager at the grocery store where you shop and demand more locally raised products. By all means, shop at farmers' markets if they have them in your city. Even in cities where farmers' markets are not available, small community markets located in parking lots or along strip malls are emerging. These tend to be open only on select days but they offer fresh fruits and vegetables usually grown on nearby farms. Local communities should band together to develop community gardens, which could be one solution to the food deserts.

Chapter 4
The Electric Car Is Here

Driving cars today is a major cause of greenhouse gases. Carbon dioxide emissions from the transportation sector were 407.5 million metric tons higher than in 1990, an increase of more than 465% in unadjusted energy-related carbon dioxide emissions from all sectors over the period.[1] When you consider the fact that 86% of us drive to work alone, the picture becomes very clear that we need to change the way we use our automobiles.[2]

Approximately 20% of the average household budget is spent on the automobile.[3] If more of us would try driving less, it would have a great impact on air quality and the decreased demand for fuel would help reduce fuel costs. We can start by sharing a ride with a friend or co-worker a few days a week; just one day a week would be a big step.

To demonstrate the point about how changing driving habits can reduce the harmful emissions generated by automobiles, we need to look at what the Chinese government did in order to prepare for the 2008 Olympics in Beijing. Knowing the world would be watching, and realizing that some athletes were concerned about training and competing in a place with such poor air quality, the Chinese government resorted to extreme measures just a few weeks before the start of the games. Several factories were ordered closed and car owners could only drive their vehicles every other day. Vehicles with a license plate ending with an odd number drove one day, and those with a license plate ending with an even number drove the next day.[4] After a week or so, news reports cited the huge visible improvement in overall air quality. Many people around the world heard or read about the results of these measures, yet they have not made any changes to their driving habits.

As Lester Brown pointed out in his book, *Plan B 2.0: Rescuing a Planet Under Stress and a Civilization in Trouble*, if China one day should have three cars for every four people, as the United States now does, its fleet would total

1.1 billion vehicles, well beyond the current world fleet of 800 million. Providing the roads, highways, and parking lots for such a fleet would require paving an area roughly equal to China's land in rice, its principal staple.[5] There will not be enough oil in the ground to sustain gas-powered automobiles in the coming years. Perhaps before we get to this point, measures even more extreme than those used by the Chinese government will be instituted to help save the environment. We've seen similar actions taken in cities in America during water shortages. Residents are limited to certain days for watering their lawns or washing cars. Limited driving days could also become a reality in America to improve air quality and to conserve fuel.

Again, if we must drive, we need to make changes from the way we are currently driving. Here are a few tips to help us improve our gas mileage:

- Install a fuel monitor on your car's dashboard so you can be aware of the fuel you use while you drive.
- Avoid quick starts—accelerate slowly with ease.
- Try to avoid unnecessary stopping and braking. Maintain a steady pace.
- Eliminate the junk in the trunk. Too much weight can strain the engine, causing greater fuel consumption.
- Plan errands and trips ahead of time to eliminate having to make extra trips.
- Get out of the car. When shopping at several stores in the same area, walk from store to store instead of driving—many of us can use the exercise.
- Run errands clockwise. United Parcel Service realized that waiting for left-hand turns increased fuel consumption and route time. The company created routes with four right-hand turns for every left turn and saved 51,000 gallons of fuel. Greenhouse gas emissions were reduced by almost 600 tons over 18 months.[6]
- Slow down—reducing speed saves fuel.

Many people are using services such as those offered by Zipcar® to satisfy their driving requirements. Zipcar is a company that rents cars by the hour or by the day. These types of services can eliminate the costs of owning a vehicle including gasoline, insurance and maintenance. Zipcars are considered easier to rent than vehicles from most traditional rental car companies.[7]

There are a lot of people who own and drive their cars only for specific trips such as to travel into town, to go to and from weekly doctor's appointments or for weekend shopping. Biking, using scooters, taking public transportation, car pooling and walking are all becoming more popular as alternatives to traditional vehicle driving. This trend is only going to increase as new and better products and services continue to emerge to address the needs of the eco-consumer. For example, elongated racks mounted on the front of the bicycles enable the rider to carry much more than the typical bike racks. Also on the market are bikes that fold and fit in a carrying satchel for easy transport. In Chicago, city transit buses have racks for a few bikes and the famous "L" (elevated train) now allows bikes on board.[8]

To make it safer and easier for more people to travel by bike or scooter or to even walk more, city officials need to pass and enforce laws to protect cyclists and pedestrians from automobiles.

Consider a Hybrid

If you are in the market for an automobile, consider a hybrid. There are differences among manufacturers, some systems having full hybrid capabilities, while others are known as mild hybrids. Depending on the driving conditions, the full hybrid vehicle runs on the best combination of:

- Gasoline engine power
- Electric motor power generated by the gasoline engine
- Electric motor power of the hybrid battery

The engine is efficiently used in the following ways:

- When stopping the vehicle, the gasoline engine is automatically stopped.
- When applying the brakes or decelerating, electricity is converted from the turning force of the wheels and stored in the hybrid battery. This is called regenerative brake.[9]

Since the battery is charged by the gasoline engine as needed, it does not require charging from an outside source like an electric vehicle. The hybrid is arguably the most popular of the eco-friendly automobiles.

I don't see many Black people driving hybrids. As gas prices will undoubtedly continue to be of concern for most drivers, the hybrid vehicle will become more popular to Black consumers. In addition to the hybrid saving money through increased fuel efficiency, the hybrid vehicle is less harmful to the environment.

Automobile companies are beginning to make the emotional connection of owning a hybrid. An example is the Ford commercial where a school-age girl is riding in an SUV with her dad. She asks her dad to drop her off a block or so from her destination because she does not want to be seen riding in a non-hybrid car. The idea is to show that there is positive peer pressure to be among the "in crowd" of people who are concerned about the environment, even among teenagers. The commercial ends with the dad telling the daughter that the vehicle they are riding in is in fact a hybrid. The daughter wonders why he never talked about it and the dad tells her that he didn't think he needed to mention it.

Whatever that emotional connection is, car companies will tap into it. For example, for many Black people the emotional connection may not be the environmental benefit right now. The emotional connection will more likely be the money-saving benefit of owning a hybrid. Adding more style to the design of these vehicles will further increase the appeal to Black consumers.

Actress Kerry Washington makes a point to have drivers pick her up in hybrids.[10] Many movie stars and entertainers have chosen hybrids for traveling to the high-profile award shows, and many of them own hybrids as well. While the hybrid vehicle is becoming more popular, automobile technology needs to get to a level where the vehicle can run entirely on electric, solar or some other renewable means. A fully electric vehicle seems to be the area of focus today for automobile manufacturers. It is interesting to note that electric cars were on the roads nearly 100 years ago and as recently as 2003 in California before they were taken off the market.[11]

Who Killed the Electric Car?

To get an idea of how a fully electric automobile operates from a consumer standpoint, the documentary film *Who Killed the Electric Car?* is a great source of information. The film focuses on the controversy surrounding electric vehicles in general and the EV1, General Motors' electric vehicle, in particular.[12] The EV1 was the first modern production electric vehicle from a major automaker in nearly 100 years. It was also the first purpose-built electric car produced by General Motors in the United States.

Introduced in 1996, the EV1 electric cars were available in California and Arizona for lease only, as well as through a Southern Company employee lease program in Georgia. These cars could be serviced at designated Saturn retailers. General Motors discontinued the EV1 after 1999 and subsequently removed all but a few of the cars from the roads in 2003. The discontinuation of the EV1 was and remains a very controversial topic.[13]

As the film illustrates, several factors led to the demise of the electric vehicle. Perhaps the most controversial factor was the Zero Emissions mandate passed by the California Air Resources Board (CARB) in 1990. The mandate stipulated that 10 percent of new vehicles sold by manufacturers must meet zero-emissions standards by 2003. CARB was sued by car companies who were convinced they could not meet the deadline. Under intense pressure, CARB killed the mandate on April 24, 2003. During the summer of 2003, the last leased EV1 was turned in.[14]

Perhaps the most engaging section of the film was where the former EV1 leasers organized vigils urging General Motors to sell them the EV1s. Rumors spread on the Internet that General Motors was planning to send the cars to its Mesa, Arizona, proving grounds. The former leasers were suspicious of what would happen to the vehicles once they arrived in Arizona. A group of former leasers flew over the grounds in a helicopter and observed the cars being stacked and crushed.[15]

Colette Divine, a Black actress, was one of those angry electric vehicle leasers featured in the documentary. She faced arrest twice during the EV1 vigil. Note her passion in an interview with EVWorld.com when asked why a woman of color was on the front lines of this issue. "We should be concerned, because people of color are like white people in that we all need to breathe air, drink clean water, live the same life as white people do. In this country, they started this term 'the environment' and I think we need to take 'the' out of it and replace it with 'our' because 'the environment' is [not] some thing like 'the mall' or, 'the gas station'. Our environment is something that sustains us and it's up to us to help sustain it, because we have a shared relationship here."

She further added, "Don't confuse a lack of representation with a lack of concern. I believe people of color are concerned with their environment. They'll be the ones who end up paying more at the gas pump and [in] economically deprived areas, certain things are more expensive. Being economically depressed leads one to being apathetic, in general, because life is just such a struggle day-to-day that the issues of trees and grass seem not as important."[16]

The EV1 perhaps was ahead of its time, and it certainly gave us a bar by which to measure future electric cars. Though the documentary asks, "Who killed the electric car?" many groups and even residents were listed among the culprits. Regardless of who killed the electric car, the need to resurrect it, or at least the technology, is imminent today and will be in the future.

Perhaps the major issue with delivering a fully electric automobile to the market today is the battery. Developing a battery that is not too heavy, that is cost effective, and can run for a considerable period of time are key issues facing car manufacturers.

Meet Shai Agassi

Shai Agassi might be the man to solve the electric vehicle battery challenges once and for all. The former head of products at SAP, the world's largest maker of enterprise software, wants to eliminate the oil consuming CO_2 cars altogether. He is not interested in short-term fixes like substituting hybrids or flex-fuel technology. He wants to eliminate cars as we have come to know them. In 2007 Agassi launched Project Better Place, the world's first global electric car grid operator. The new concept he proposed is called the Electric Recharge Grid Operator (ERGO). The ERGO would replace traditional gas stations by covering an entire country with a network of "smart" charge locations. Drivers could then plug in and get a charge anywhere by subscribing to a specific plan—like cell phones. Different plans would allow drivers the option to pay as they go or unlimited miles, all for less than the equivalent cost of gas. Cars could be purchased from operators who would offer deep discounts or perhaps even give the cars away. The profit would be generated from selling electricity.[17]

With each new concept like the one Shai Agassi is proposing, we get closer to the reality of fully electric vehicles on our roads. While the EV1 was among the electric cars that were swept off the streets in 2003, the film featured a commercial that introduced the car, pondering how such a vehicle could run without gas, air, sparks, transmission, etc. The commercial ended by pro-

Chapter 5
Invoking Green in Education

Many inner-city schools, attended by a majority of Black children, are plagued with problems including a near 50% dropout rate and failure to meet testing standards.[1] A green curriculum could be just the thing to create some excitement among our inner-city youth to get them interested in education.

Start with your children's school principal and volunteer to help the school go green even if you're not well versed in green initiatives yourself. Schools generate a lot of waste, especially in the cafeteria. Each day boxes, cans, plastic, and paper associated with food packaging are thrown away, in addition to the food itself. Every day school cafeterias waste tons of fruit. In Chicago's public schools, a piece of fruit is required for each lunch serving in an effort to provide a balanced meal. Many of these apples, oranges, and bananas go directly into the garbage. These uneaten pieces of fruit can help make nutrient-rich compost.* Fruit is just a start. The compost can be added to the school yard's soil and used in school gardens that the students can maintain themselves. The schools could also sell the compost to residents in the local community to help raise funds for various programs. In fact, there are organizations that provide grants for student gardening initiatives.

All of the milk and juice cartons and the cardboard boxes and cans used to package the food can be recycled too. As you begin to make inroads into the waste situation at the schools, you can bring attention to the need for organic food in the schools. The documentary, *Super Size Me*, shows how organic food in schools does not cost significantly more than the food currently served in school lunch programs.[2]

Adding compact fluorescent lights, reducing the use of and reusing paper and other supplies, and regulating heating and cooling will help the school go green while further reducing costs.

See page 7.

Teach Green

School administrators and teachers should start including green projects in the curriculum. Green topics could be included in every subject and introduced to children at all grade levels—the younger the better. If our five-year-old daughter can teach us what to do during a fire based on what she learned in school, she can learn and teach us about turning off lights and not letting the water run while we brush our teeth. For the older students, subjects such as science and biology should focus heavily on green, with the annual science fair promoting green entries that would be awarded extra credit. Invite local business owners to serve as judges so that they too can become educated about the environment and motivated to help with local green initiatives.

The Historically Black Colleges and Universities / Black Farmer Initiative

Black colleges are a key institution in the Black community. Black colleges historically were the only means of higher education afforded Black people. There is an endless list of nationally and internationally recognized Blacks in every area of study, sports, and entertainment who graduated or studied at Historically Black Colleges and Universities (HBCUs).

Today, HBCUs could play a pivotal role in helping to ensure the survival of Black-owned farms. The number of Black farms across the nation is rapidly dwindling. At the turn of the century, there were more than a million of these farms in America. Today there are just over 18,000 Black-owned farms identified by the U.S. Department of Agriculture.[3] Systemic discrimination against Black farmers has had a devastating effect, contributing to this rapid decline.

Many HBCUs are located in the South where 50% of all Black people live today and where many of the Black farms are located.[4] The HBCUs could partner with local Black farmers to supply food to the HBCUs. In exchange for the food, the HBCUs could provide agricultural assistance and education to the farmers. This could include teaching the farmers eco-friendly farming techniques and helping them establish new markets for their organic products. HBCUs should increase the scholarships offered to students who are interested in studying agriculture and farming. As the world approaches a global food shortage, we need to be involved in the solution to this challenge, implementing food and agriculture initiatives, especially since poor people are the ones most affected in such crises.

HBCUs That Could Lead the Partnership

The HBCUs that are poised to lead this partnership are those universities that have agriculture as part of their mission. These universities are called land-grant institutions of higher education and have been designated by the U.S. Congress to receive the benefits of the *Morrill Acts of 1862 and 1890.*[5] The Morrill Act of

1862 was also known as the Land-Grant College Act. It was a major boost to higher education in America. The grant was originally set up to establish institutions in each state that would educate people in agriculture, home economics, mechanical arts, and other professions that were practical at the time.

The Land Grant College Act was introduced by Vermont Congressman Justin Morrill. He envisioned the financing of agricultural and mechanical education and wanted to assure that education would be available to those in all social classes.

The first Morrill Act made no reference to color, which allowed southern states to deny access to minorities. To address this inequity, Congress passed the Second Morrill Act, which specified that states that maintained separate colleges for different races had to propose a just and equitable division of the funds to be received under the act. Any states that had used their 1862 funds entirely for the education of White students were forced to either open their facilities to Black students or to provide separate facilities for them. This act served to establish sixteen Black land-grant colleges throughout the South. These universities became known as "The 1890 Land-Grant Institutions." Each of those southern states that did not have a Black college by 1890 established one later under the Second Morrill Act.

Tuskegee Institute was created by an act of the Alabama Legislature. Twelve years later, however, the state established and incorporated a Board of Trustees and named the school private. Thus, it is not a land-grant college, in spite of the fact that it was granted 25,000 acres of land by the United States Congress in 1899. The triple-mission of the land-grant institutions is the concept of research, instruction, and extension service.[6] For more than 100 years, these institutions have provided educational opportunities to Black people and others who were excluded from higher education.

Obviously, these institutions can play a vital role in ensuring the longevity of the Black farmer. Currently, there are eighteen land-grant HBCUs:

Alabama A&M University	Prairie View A&M University
Alcorn State University	South Carolina State University
Delaware State University	Southern University
Florida A&M University	Tennessee State University
Fort Valley State University	Tuskegee University
Kentucky State University	University of Arkansas-Pine Bluff
Langston University	University of Maryland Eastern Shore
Lincoln University	Virginia State University
North Carolina A&T State University	West Virginia State University[7]

Biofuel Exploration and the Black Farmer

With the focus on cleaner alternatives to gasoline, there is a rapid move in America to produce ethanol. Trains are now transporting corn, the new cash crop, to support the production of ethanol. Corn-based ethanol is not much cheaper than gasoline when you consider the resources needed to grow, to process and to transport the end product. However, Black farmers should still be a part of the process to develop a more efficient biofuel. The best lobbyists to ensure that Black farmers get a seat at the table are Black elected officials. State senators, congressmen, and other elected officials should ensure that Black farmers participate in all clean alternative fuel initiatives, as well as any other new mass-scale energy programs.

HBCUs should establish "going green" as a major platform in the college president's strategic plan. Faculty members might have a "green" objective as part of their employee evaluation. At the student level, every degree program might have a required green course.

Going green would save operating costs and improve the overall quality of campus life. Black college students are among the Black demographic called key influencers and early adopters. Just as they heavily influence the music we listen to, the clothes we wear, and the cars we drive, they can speed up the adoption of a green lifestyle by making it cool. If a brother or sister says something is cool. . . . it's cool! Green is cool.

Meet Tuskegee University's Green Giant

> Tuskegee University has a rich history in being green with one of the most famous pioneers in agriculture the world has known.
>
> George Washington Carver (1864-1943) was an American botanical researcher and agronomy educator who worked in the agricultural extension at the Tuskegee Institute (now Tuskegee University) in Tuskegee, Alabama. Carver taught former slaves farming techniques for self-sufficiency.
>
> To bring education to farmers, Carver designed a mobile school. In 1921, he spoke in favor of a peanut tariff before the U.S. House of Representatives Ways and Means Committee. Given the racial discrimination of the time, it was most unusual for a Black American to be called an expert. Carver's well-received testimony earned him national attention, and he became an unofficial spokesman for the peanut industry. Carver wrote forty-four practical agricultural bulletins for farmers. In the post-Civil War South, a monoculture of cotton had depleted the soil, and in the early 1900s, the boll weevil destroyed the majority of the cotton crop. Much of Carver's fame was based on his research and promotion of alternative crops, such as peanuts and sweet potatoes. He wanted farmers to grow alternative crops as both a source of their own food and as cash crops. His most popular bulletin contained over one hundred food recipes that used peanuts. He also created about a hundred existing industrial products from peanuts, including cosmetics, paints, dyes, plastics, gasoline, and nitroglycerine. Carver's most important accomplishments were in areas other than industrial products from peanuts, including agricultural extension education, improvement of racial relations, advocacy of sustainable agriculture, and the appreciation of plants and nature.[8]

Clearly, George Washington Carver understood the importance of reuse, and he knew a thing or two about creating and developing new markets for products. Perhaps most importantly, he educated others on how to do the same.

Tuskegee University continues its rich farming history today through its College of Agricultural, Environmental, and Natural Sciences (CAENS). The university's Alabama Small Farm Rural Economic Development Center works with several partner agencies, including the USDA, the State of Alabama Department of Agriculture and Industries; Resource Conservation and Development Councils, the Alabama Indian Affairs Commissions, and private entrepreneurs and farmers. Tuskegee's Small Farm Center has targeted rural community development efforts including farm-related, value-added, wholesale / retail, community-based mini-grant projects, and rural infrastructures.[9]

Colleges Making the Green Grade

Williams College in Massachusetts had a green commencement in 2007. The food served included locally produced fresh cinnamon gelato, organic greens, and fresh asparagus. Disposable plates and cutlery were replaced with eco-friendly options. Even the paper napkins and straws were biodegradable.[10]

At Harvard, the call to go green starts before incoming freshmen set foot on campus. Incoming freshmen receive communication urging them to bring CFLs and to buy only energy-efficient refrigerators. Harvard also pays 20 undergraduate students to help fellow students go green in fun ways. Efforts include dormitory competitions to win the Green Cup for the greatest energy reductions and largest increases in recycling. One day each year, students pile trash collected from Harvard Yard into a huge heap called Mount Trashmore. The trash monument serves as a reminder to students of how much they are throwing away—and how much waste they could avoid by recycling.[11]

Atlanta's Spelman College is the first HBCU to build a LEED-certified residence hall. The Leadership in Energy and Environmental Design (LEED) Green Building Rating System is a voluntary, consensus-based national rating system for developing high-performance sustainable buildings. LEED addresses all building types and emphasizes state-of-the-art strategies in five areas: sustainable site development, water savings, energy efficiency, materials and resources selection, and indoor environmental quality. The certification levels include LEED Certified, LEED Certified Silver, Gold and Platinum. Spelman's 200,000 square-foot structure combines environmental-friendly design with innovation and is designated LEED Certified Silver.[12]

Connecticut College publishes an environmental handbook for its students. The introduction in the handbook sets the tone for how serious the college is about saving the environment: "This booklet is designed to provide Connecticut College community members with recommendations for energy conservation, waste reduction and recycling best management practices for common hazardous materials and information on campus environmental groups and activities. This is most important at Connecticut College because, like other colleges and universities, we are a microcosm of society. We house and feed people, consume energy, maintain facilities, purchase goods and services and administer projects. Sustainable living, i.e., minimizing resource use and waste production, benefits us environmentally, economically and socially."

The campus boasts an Environmental Model Committee comprised of dedicated students, faculty, and staff; Building and House Environmental Representatives; and more. Small steps, such as turning a light off when leaving an unoccupied room or turning off the computer when you're going to be away for more than fifteen minutes can save energy. When multiplied by many, the savings become greater.[13]

The green movement is going to continue to grow. If the Black community is going to be a part of, and benefit from, this growth, we need to be educated about green. HBCUs must become actively engaged in the discourse of going green.

Chapter 6
Cashing In on Green

Perhaps one of the best reasons why the Black community should embrace the green movement is the number of jobs that are being created now and will be in the future. In any given city in America, unemployment in the Black community is usually double the national average, especially among Black men. When the Black man is unable to find work, the effects on the family are devastating. Often times in other ethnic groups there are various options within the family that can temporarily tide a family over until they are able to get back on their feet. In the Black community such options are not usually available. In Greensburg, Kansas, Daniel Wallach, director of a sustainable energy organization, told me, "People can only get so excited about a $20.00 savings on their utility bill. What you really have to do to get a community to seriously embrace green initiatives is to find the need of that community and solve it."[1] In the Black community, that need is jobs.

Green Jobs

A new Green-Collar Jobs report from the nonprofit American Solar Energy Society (ASES) shows that as many as one out of four workers in the United States will be working in the renewable energy or energy efficiency industries by 2030. According to ASES, this is the nation's first comprehensive report on the size and growth of the renewable energy and energy efficiency industries. The report shows that these industries already generate 8.5 million jobs in the United States. The report adds that, with appropriate public policy, there could be as many as 40 million jobs by 2030.[2] In a press release from the ASES, director of marketing Neal Lurie said, "The green collar job boom is here. Everyone knew that renewable energy and energy efficiency are good for the environment, but we now know they are economic powerhouses too."[3] Key findings of the report included:

- By the year 2030, the renewable energy and energy efficiency industries could generate up to $4.5 trillion in revenue in the United States, but only if we develop the appropriate public policy, including a renewable portfolio standard, renewable energy incentives, public education, and R&D.
- The 40 million jobs that could be created in the renewable energy and energy efficiency industries by 2030 are not just engineering-related, but also include millions of new jobs in manufacturing, construction, accounting, and management.
- The renewable energy and energy efficiency industries today generate nearly $1 trillion in revenue in the United States, contributing more than $150 billion in tax revenue at the federal, state, and local levels.
- The revenue from the energy efficiency sector—including revenues from energy-efficient windows, appliances, insulation, and recycling—is currently larger than the revenue from renewable energy, but the renewable energy industry is growing at a faster rate.
- Solar, wind, ethanol, and fuel cells are likely to be some of the hottest areas of growth.[4]

Lester Brown, an expert on environmental economics, cites other growth industries needed to build a new, eco-friendly economy in his book *Plan B 2.0: Rescuing a Planet Under Stress and a Civilization in Trouble.* Among the many changes in world food economy will be the continuing shift to fish farming. The farming of fish, particularly omnivorous species such as carp and tilapia, is likely to continue expanding rapidly simply because these fish convert grain into animal protein so efficiently.

Bicycle manufacturing and service is a growth industry. As recently as 1965, world production of cars and bikes was essentially the same, with each at nearly 20 million. However, in 2003, bike production topped over 100 million per year compared with 43 million cars.

Yet another growth industry is raising water productivity. Just as the last half-century was devoted to raising land productivity, this half-century will be focused on raising water productivity. Irrigation technologies will become more efficient. The continuous recycling of urban water supplies, already started in some cities, will become common, replacing the "flush and forget" system.

As oil prices rise, we are already seeing teleconferencing gaining appeal. To save fuel and time, individuals will be attending more conferences electronically with both audio and visual connections.[5] Telecommuting and home office jobs are also becoming more common.

Other promising growth industries are light rail construction and tree planting. There is also a growing demand for environmental architects who can design buildings that are energy- and material-efficient and that maximize natural heating, cooling, and lighting.[6]

Meet Van Jones

Van Jones is the founder and president of Green for All, based in Oakland, California. The mission of Green for All is to help build an inclusive, green economy—strong enough to lift millions of people out of poverty. Van is a tireless advocate, championing "green-collar jobs and opportunities" for disadvantaged people. He is committed to creating "green pathways out of poverty," while greatly expanding the coalition fighting global warming.

In 2007, Van helped the City of Oakland pass a "Green Jobs Corps" proposal; the city allocated funds to train Oakland residents in eco-friendly "green-collar jobs."

At the national level, Van worked successfully in 2007 with U.S. House of Representatives Speaker Nancy Pelosi, Senator Hillary Clinton, Senator Bernie Sanders, U.S. Rep. Hilda Solis and U.S. Rep. John Tierney to pass the Green Jobs Act of 2007. That path breaking, historic legislation authorized $125 million in funding to train 35,000 people a year in "green-collar jobs."

Van is also a co-founder of a new national coalition that promotes the idea of a national "Clean Energy Jobs Corps." This multibillion-dollar federal initiative would put hundreds of thousands of people to work rewiring and retrofitting the energy infrastructure of the United States.

A 1993 Yale Law graduate, Van is proud to champion some of the most hopeful solutions to America's toughest challenges.[7]

Jobs created by the green economy could help reduce the high unemployment levels and revitalize our neighborhoods. We need to embrace green so that we can become knowledgeable about emerging industries, jobs, and new technology. Thanks to Van Jones, Neal Lurie, and Lester Brown, and men like them, the word is getting out on how the future looks bright—for green job growth.

Green Investing

More and more people are not only doing the right thing by being environmentally conscious, but they are also beginning to spend money with companies that are conscious about the environment. Socially responsible investing (SRI), also known as sustainable investing or ethical investing, has become popular. The SRI strategy seeks to maximize both financial return and social good.

In general, socially responsible investors favor corporate best practices that promote environmental stewardship, consumer protection, human rights, and diversity. Some (but not all) avoid businesses involved in alcohol, tobacco, gambling, weapons, the military, and abortion.[8]

Similarly, the Advocacy Investing strategy, developed by Marc J. Lane Investment Management, Inc., is a new development in the socially responsible or principle-focused segment of the total U.S. investment pool. This segment has become very significant: principle-focused investments rose more than 324 percent from $639 billion in 1995 to $2.71 trillion in 2007 to become 10 percent of the $25.1 trillion in investment assets under professional management by major financial institutions.[9]

(As reported in the 2007 Report on Socially Responsible Investing Trends in the United States, Social Investment Forum.)

In the Advocacy Investing approach, the investment manager first screens for sound business fundamentals and corporate governance and seeks to identify companies whose corporate behavior reflects and promotes an investor's personal beliefs and values. These may relate to such social concerns as the company's practices regarding the environment by looking at areas such as recycling efforts or pollution control, or such issues as human rights and diversity. Once these steps are complete, a diversified portfolio is built around companies whose approaches to conducting business are consistent with the core principles that the investor advocates.

In contrast, Socially Responsible Investing first builds a portfolio and then, based on the guidelines of the portfolio, uses a negative screen excluding from the investment portfolio socially controversial industries such as tobacco, alcohol, gambling, defense, and adult entertainment, along with industries associated with pollution or depletion of natural resources, such as mining and energy.[10]

What is Advocacy Investing? Copyright 2008. Marc J. Lane Investment Management, Inc. Reprinted with permission.

Advocacy Investing is a trademark of Marc J. Lane Investment Management, Inc. registered in the U.S. Patent and Trademark Office and may be registered in other jurisdictions.

Chapter 7
Black Institutions That Should Be Green

Another way to propel the green movement in our community is to have key institutions and leaders issue the call. Institutions like the Black church and colleges, along with political leaders and business people, have served as the life- line for Black people throughout our sojourn in this country. Pioneers in these and other areas opened the door and helped pave the way to progress for our people. Today, these institutions and leaders are needed to help motivate Black people to go green.

Black Cities That Need to Go Green

At the beginning of this book, I cited a "vicious cycle" referred to by Malcolm X in describing the neighborhoods we lived in during the sixties. Currently, in almost any city in America, Black neighborhoods tend to have those same problems that perpetuate the cycle: high unemployment, crime, drugs, and a host of health problems including HIV AIDS, alcoholism, diabetes, and obesity. If our homes, blocks, neighborhoods, and cities go green, many of these problems would go away. Let's take a look at a few predominantly Black cities and highlight "why" and "how" they can go green.

Detroit, Michigan

In the post-Mayor Coleman Young era, the city of Detroit has heard themes of revival and renewal with each mayoral election. Although some progress has been made, many citizens feel the progress is taking too long as crime, unemployment, and the lack of real opportunities for many inner-city Blacks remain. Additionally, Detroit ranks among the "most obese cities" in the United States.[1]

Detroit is a city that needs green like it was going out of style. I have three recommendations for the city of Detroit to go green:

1. Start a citywide community health initiative, *Operation Trim the Fat,* to encourage the citizens to lose a few pounds. Detroit consistently ranks near the top of the list of the "Fattest Cities in America," according to *Men's Fitness Magazine.*[2] City officials could lead the charge to mobilize the "Motor City" in a non-automotive way. Going green should improve overall health as people walk and bike more instead of driving. And eating organic and healthier food definitely will help improve their health.

2. Provide automobile and other manufacturers and their suppliers with incentives to go green. With its mass production facilities turning out cars, Detroit uses an enormous amount of resources to manufacture those automobiles. Let us not forget the enormous amount of waste created from the excess packaging for the tons of products and materials needed to support the automobile manufacturing industry. Reducing the amount of energy needed to manufacture automobiles by using alternative or renewable energy sources would help save the environment and save money. If the manufacturing sector of the massive automotive industry can go green, they obviously can make more affordable environmentally friendly automobiles.

3. Provide incentives for people to purchase hybrid and other eco-friendly vehicles. Illinois now offers a $1,000.00 tax credit for new hybrid car purchases. Detroit and the state of Michigan can do the same.[3]

By going green, new technologies will emerge and new jobs will be created. This will help reduce the high rate of unemployment in Detroit, especially among young Black men.

"Hotlanta"—Atlanta, Georgia

Atlanta, the Black Mecca of the South, is a booming city. Atlanta is rich in civil rights history and has arguably the largest concentration of Black college students in the world with Spellman, Morehouse, and Clark Atlanta. Driving in and around Atlanta, however, is a major challenge, as Atlanta ranks fifth among America's "Worst Commutes" according to the Urban Mobility Report.[4]

It is impressive to see successful brothers and sisters, inside or outside the perimeter of metro Atlanta, driving the slick Jaguars, convertible BMWs, Lexus, Mercedes-Benzes, and other luxury rides—wheeling and dealing as the next generation of movers and shakers. However, the emissions spewed from hundreds of thousands of cars every day is part of the reason Atlanta ranked among the top cities for respiratory problems. According to the American Lung

Association's website, Atlanta ranks in the top "25 Most Ozone-Polluted Cities".[5] Even with a state-of-the-art rapid transit system, most people still use their cars for the daily commute. City officials should organize a Metropolitan Atlanta Rapid Transit Authority (MARTA) Day encouraging citizens to ride the commuter trains to work. Special fares could provide incentives.

An environmental glimmer of hope rests with an exciting initiative called The BeltLine. Since Atlanta ranks near the bottom of United States peer cities in terms of the amount of available parkland, the BeltLine proposal will increase green space in a connected linear system that would become, in effect, one of the nation's great regional parks. The BeltLine can add new green space, mixed-use developments, and neighborhood connectivity to Atlanta. The BeltLine will create a linear park that connects 40 of Atlanta's parks, including over 1,200 acres of new green space and improvements to approximately 700 acres of existing green space.

As in every great city, increased green space will be a major driver for economic development. Mixed-use communities (some combination of residential, business, industrial, etc.,) will be attracted to the linear park and new park acreage. The BeltLine's park system will be as important as its railroads, streetscapes, and other infrastructure in determining the location and concentration of development in Atlanta. Key elements of the BeltLine include streetscapes, jobs, green space, parks, trails, environmental cleanup, historic preservation, and transit.[6]

New Orleans, Louisiana

With all the rebuilding after Hurricane Katrina, emphasis should be placed on green construction throughout the city of New Orleans. This is a golden opportunity for neighborhoods across the city to implement many of the initiatives discussed in this book. Hollywood entertainers, professional athletes, corporations, churches, civic groups, and citizens across the country have all given money, time, and resources to help rebuild New Orleans. The "Crescent City" can roll out a green initiative that includes the Mississippi River, the controversial dams, and the countless other problem areas that led to that tragic event in September 2005.

What Hurricane Katrina should've taught us.

Much has been said about Hurricane Katina, so I won't rehash it here. Hurricane Katrina was not only a tremendous natural disaster, it was racially polarizing. I agree with those who argue that had the victims of the hurricane been overwhelmingly White, the government would have had a more expeditious response team. Moreover, I feel that Hurricane Katrina should be the wake-up call we need in the Black community on several fronts, including disaster preparedness, available emergency funds, food, and community organization.

Imagine being stranded, as the people were in New Orleans, and even if you had money in the bank, or in your pocket for that matter, you still couldn't get access to food. Could you go one or two or three days without food? We should take a look at our daily food consumption and start to reduce our portions and overall food intake. If we condition ourselves to eat less, we might be able to function better in a rare situation when we may not have access to food.

A friend of mine told me a long time ago that periodically throughout the year he and his family go on a self-imposed austerity program, when they eat beans, rice, and bread for one week. We have adopted this in our household, although not as often. What we have learned, or at least have tried to stress to our children, is that we can live on less. We live in a country that wastes so much.

An article in the *Final Call* newspaper highlighted the fact that Black people are not prepared for major disasters. The article cited that this could be based on a lack of funding for programs to help prepare communities for disasters along with a lack of understanding by Black people about the importance of planning and being ready.[7] We tend to be a reaction-based people who are quick to say, "If I coulda, woulda, shoulda." We don't want to live through the aftermath of another disaster like Katrina.

Notable Green Cities

There are a number of cities that are viewing green as a way to save on energy costs while helping the environment at the same time. As more cities achieve success, hopefully other cities will begin to adopt similar initiatives. Most inner cities struggle with trying to provide adequate services because there never seems to be enough money in the budget. Although, as most of us know, a budget is often wasted on inefficient services and departments. Going green is invoking new energy in cities, which should make citizens take pride in where they live. Here are a few examples of some cities demonstrating green, forward thinking.

Washington D.C.—A Potential Model Green City

The District boasts being one of the greenest cities in the country. In September 2007, the District of Columbia announced two major environmental initiatives aimed at building up the District's workforce and encouraging transit use, highlighting the city's position as a national leader for environmental policies and sustainable development.

Plans include naming a Green-Collar Jobs Advisory Council that will involve members of the mayor's administration, nonprofit and advocacy organizations, contractors, and developers. The Council will devise a strategy for linking the District's green building policies to job creation. Beginning in 2008, the District began requiring all new government buildings to go green. By 2012, all new buildings larger than 50,000 square feet—public or private—must conform to green standards. The Advisory Council will determine how the

District can prepare its workforce to participate in the green building boom—from high school apprenticeship programs to graduate degrees.[8]

Mayor Fenty, who is an avid biker, has established annual Car-Free Days in the District to encourage residents and visitors to use alternate means of transportation. More than a third of the city's residents already take public transit to work—a higher percentage than any other city except New York. Another 13% of residents choose to bike or walk.[9]

Chicago, Illinois

Chicago is trying to become the "greenest city in America." The city has planted 500,000 trees, invested hundreds of millions of dollars in the revitalization of parks and neighborhoods, and added more than two million square feet of rooftop gardens—more than anywhere else in the United States. Also, many of the transit buses are now hybrids.[10]

San Francisco, California

San Francisco has banned all plastic bags. Fifty years ago, plastic bags, starting first with the sandwich bag, were seen in the United States as a more sanitary and environmentally friendly alternative to the deforesting paper bag. Now, an estimated 180 million plastic bags are distributed to shoppers each year in San Francisco. Made of filmy plastic, they are hard to recycle and easily blow into trees and waterways, where they are blamed for killing marine life. They also occupy much-needed landfill space.[11] One of my favorite cities, San Francisco, has said no to plastic bags.

Seattle, Washington

Seattle has been a driving force in the area of climate protection. The Emerald City has committed to meeting the carbon emissions-reduction goals called for in the Kyoto climate treaty and has inspired more than 500 other mayors across the country to make that same pledge.[12]

Vote Green

The aforementioned cities have been highlighted for their mayoral leadership and others are implementing green initiatives. We need to make sure that existing and future elected officials are green conscious. We can do this with our vote. Just as the call to "go to school and get a good education" is a common issue among Black people, the call to "get out and vote" is another issue that ranks high among our people. In every election, candidates, both White and Black, call on the Black church to help mobilize the ever-important Black vote. Voting continues to be one of those areas where emotions run high within the Black community. We are constantly reminded that our ancestors died for the right to vote.

Historically, the Republican Party, the party of Lincoln, was considered the favored party among Black people; today the Democratic Party is the overwhelming party of choice. Black people consistently give their vote to the Democratic Party without question and, in most cases, without requiring anything in return. This must stop. We need to begin demanding something in return for our votes and the implementation of green initiatives should be among our demands.

We should ask our candidates to define their green agenda and explain how that agenda reaches the inner city where most Black people live. If they cannot articulate specific actions to help save the environment and create green jobs in the process, they do not deserve our votes. Remember, you can vote with your wallet by buying products that are environmentally friendly and with your ballot by choosing candidates who are committed to saving the environment.

Greening Congress

In 2007, House Speaker Nancy Pelosi announced plans to make the House of Representatives a model of sustainability. Her goal is to reduce energy consumption in the House by half in 10 years and reach carbon neutrality in 18 months. To accomplish this she is seeking to replace the 50 cars used by the House with hybrids, installing an ethanol pump in the garage, and adding bike racks. Installing more energy-efficient ventilation, consolidating computer servers, and converting 100% of the electricity supply to renewable sources are also included in her energy-saving plans.[13] Speaker Pelosi is setting a good example by going green on Capitol Hill.

The Black Church Needs to Go Green

If there is one thing we do as a people, it's go to church. If there was only one institution we could support, it would be the church. Black people are the most religious people on the planet, yet we have not found a way to convert that "religiosity" into some meaningful, visible, sustainable, economic progress. Instead of competing to see which mega-star Black preacher is going to build the next mega-church, the church should be the community epicenter for green. A popular question or topic of discussion among Black people today is "What would Jesus do?" I am of the belief that Jesus would preach "green."

Is there really a need to print a weekly church bulletin and calendar of events? Almost all church members have access to a computer to receive this information via email or to access it on the church Website. You might think this is trivial, but think of all the churches that print bulletins every week. Let's save some trees. Since many of us don't attend church in the same neighborhood where we live, can some of the physical church meetings be conducted via teleconference? Again, with fuel prices always being a concern, two to three trips per week for various meetings along with driving to and from work increases fuel costs and also emissions into the air.

The Black church has a responsibility to take a leadership role in saving the environment. With all the money that Black churches deposit into banks across the country every Monday morning, they can actually influence banks and other financial institutions to be "green conscious." These same banks and financial institutions could provide financial incentives such as low-interest loans for eco-friendly church renovations or for new construction of green homes and buildings.

Black Churches That Can Lead the Green Movement

In order to get more churches to adopt green initiatives, some of the more popular Black congregations should take the lead. In addition to having live broadcasts of Sunday services, these churches tend to have community outreach programs such as prison ministries, soup kitchens, after school and teenage-focused programs. There are too many nationally recognized churches and leaders to mention here but all of these organizations should be going green, including the following:

Salem Baptist Church—Chicago, Illinois

With its popular leader, Reverend James Meeks, Salem Baptist Church should assume leadership in the green movement. After all, the congregation has been mobilized to "get out the vote," to help elect none other than Jesse Jackson, Jr., to the U.S. Congress; his wife, Sandy Jackson, to the Chicago City Council; and Reverend Meeks himself as a state senator, who considered a possible run for governor. As a protégé under Jesse Jackson, Sr., Reverend Meeks has learned well. With the ability to bring out this show of force, it should be easy to get the congregation to "go green."

Abyssinian Baptist Church—New York, New York

Abyssinian Baptist Church is another ideal church for the green movement. Reverend Calvin Butts is also nationally known and is not shy when it comes to speaking out on issues of injustice. Among the church's resources is the Abyssinian Development Corporation (ADC). According to its Website, the ADC is a leading nonprofit community development corporation dedicated to building the human, social, and physical capital of Harlem. ADC offers services to the community through the following programs:

- Affordable Housing
- Family Services
- Economic Revitalization
- Education and Youth
- Civic Engagement[14]

These programs provide opportunities to invoke green initiatives. Abyssinian Baptist Church can jump on the green bandwagon already started by New York City Mayor Michael Bloomberg.

West Angeles Church of God in Christ—Los Angeles, California

With over 20,000 members, West Angeles Church of God in Christ is the largest Pentecostal church in the country.[15] Bishop Charles E. Blake presides over a congregation that includes famous members such as Earvin "Magic" Johnson, Angela Bassett, Stevie Wonder, and Denzel Washington. The church already has an extensive community outreach program. With the physical, intellectual, and financial resources available to a congregation of this size, the impact of going green would be enormous and would obviously affect Crenshaw Boulevard, the heart of the Black community in Los Angeles, where the church is located.

"Your" Church

Again, going green starts with you and, in this case, your church or religious organization. It doesn't matter how large or how small the congregation, every effort to save the environment helps. Think of ways you and your church can save the environment. Imagine the energy used to make choir robes—are they needed? As you marvel at those beautiful stained-glass windows, especially during the hot summer months, imagine those windows open with fresh air flowing into the church instead of using the air conditioner.

When it comes to transportation, it's not uncommon for a church to own a bus or van to transport members—this is a great idea. When it's time for a new vehicle, consider a hybrid. Church ministers all over the country should organize task forces within their congregations to continuously monitor ways to reduce, reuse and recycle everything in the church.

Elijah Muhammad Did It!

> *For a great example of how to put this philosophy into action, we need look no further than to the program of Elijah Muhammad. At a time when Black people were protesting for the right to eat in segregated restaurants, Elijah Muhammad was purchasing farmland in Georgia, Michigan, and Alabama, where he raised cattle and chickens and grew organic fruits and vegetables. The chickens walked on mesh wire above the ground to prevent them from eating excrement—he wanted the best for his people. Today, that would qualify as "organic extra" chickens—ensuring that everything the chickens ate was nutritional. In fact, his cattle were only exposed to chemicals when they were poisoned in Alabama in 1970, destroying over half the herd. While he was being self-sufficient and green, there was an element in Montgomery and throughout the South that didn't take too kindly to Blacks showing independence.*
>
> *He hired Black men and women to farm the land and purchased meat processing plants and trucks to haul the goods to supermarkets he purchased. And to clear up any confusion about who the real owners of these supermarkets were, he named them "Your Supermarket." He even contracted with the government of Peru and imported millions of pounds of whiting fish, which his followers sold house to house in inner-city neighborhoods across the country in the early '70s. He didn't stop there. He purchased restaurants in the Black communities, which usually included a bakery.*[16]
>
> *Years ago, when I was in graduate school, I learned about vertical integration. Vertical integration occurs when several steps in the production and/or distribution of a product or service is controlled by a single business or company. Elijah Muhammad mastered vertical integration long before the term was known in the Black community. The Black church and other groups do not have to look any further than the model he successfully implemented and then try to follow that same model. Now that would really be something to shout about—can I get an Amen?*

Greening the Black Family Reunion

I don't know of any other ethnic group that has more family reunions than Black people. Family reunions became popular after the broadcast of the miniseries *Roots*, which sparked interest among our people to trace our lineage in an effort to learn more about where we came from. Family reunions are common in most of our families, whether among siblings and their immediate families or entire family groups. Great distances are traveled to attend these events, which usually last from Friday until Sunday. Banquets, picnics, and tours of the city are among the common activities. Let's take a closer look at some key events of the family reunion to demonstrate why and how they can go green.

The Picnic

The picnic is one of the highlights of the weekend. There is usually plenty of food and beverages, which means there are a lot of paper plates, napkins, cups, aluminum cans, and water bottles. Eco-friendly paper plates and napkins are available, which organizers should use. Instead of using plastic water bottles, large water coolers can be used with the newer, environmentally friendly cups. Designate a green cleanup team to collect and separate trash and other material for recycling. Chances are there is a family member who is knowledgeable about saving the environment. This designee should be given time on the agenda to discuss green initiatives within the family on a broader scale. Family members who have traveled from across the country can take this information back to their cities and homes.

T-shirts, Caps, and Other Paraphernalia

You might think that 100 caps and t-shirts for your reunion is no big deal. But when you consider the thousands of families that order these items every year, the amount of energy used to produce these materials, along with the dyes and pesticides, it is significant. Really, is there a need for these same items year after year? Particularly when family members will most likely wear the caps and shirts only one time, which is during that weekend? Here's an idea: Why not box up all those old family reunion t-shirts and send them to various African consulates to distribute throughout the continent of Africa in an effort to connect with our long lost family members. If the t-shirts are to be keepsakes, they definitely should be made with eco-friendly material such as organic cotton, hemp, or bamboo.

The Banquet

Usually held in a large hotel banquet hall, the banquet dinner is one of the highest costs of the weekend. There is usually more food than can be consumed—creating a lot of waste. Consider eliminating the hotel banquet and, if there is still a desire to have such a dinner, consider a local facility. This could be perhaps at a community center or at a local church to save money. Organic food can be purchased and catered, or it can be prepared by family members.

At the end of the three-day celebration, a lot of resources will have been consumed and a lot of waste will have been generated. Placing a green emphasis on family reunions not only saves valuable energy during the reunion, it also heightens the awareness about the need to reduce, reuse, and recycle to a collective group of people. Again, family members will have traveled from all over the country. If, in the midst of a family weekend of fellowship, they gain an appreciation for saving the environment, hats off to the "green" family.

Chapter 8
Bury Me Green

Throughout this book, the focus has been on identifying ways in which we all can help save the environment. And hopefully, once our time on this earth is done, we can feel good about the efforts we made. But it doesn't have to stop there. We can go green even as we rest in peace.

A friend of mine tells a story of what his father often said to him, "Son, when I die, just throw me into the river." Well we don't have to go quite that far, but there are simple, yet dignified environmentally friendly ways to lay our loved ones to rest. Not only are the chemicals used for embalming harmful to the earth, but we also have to consider the high costs of funerals. Having lost a mother, a father, and three siblings within five years, I have become all too familiar with the funeral business. The average costs of a funeral can range anywhere from $3,000 to $10,000.[1] Here is a list of the typical funeral service charges, not including costs for cemetery and burial.

Average Funeral Costs

Professional Services

Basic Services of Funeral Director Staff	750.00
Embalming	645.00
Other Preparation of Body	<u>373.00</u>
	1,768.00

Facilities, Equipment and Staff

Use of Facilities and Staff for Viewing/Visitation	165.00
Use of Chapel or Set-up Fee for Church	<u>325.00</u>
	490.00

Transportation

Transfer of Remains to Funeral Home	325.00
Hearse	<u>325.00</u>
	650.00

Other Services

Saturday Service Fee	275.00
Casket	250.00
Acknowledgements	20.00
Register Book	20.00
Pallbearers' Gloves	20.00
Musician	80.00
	665.00

Total   **$3,573.00[2]**

In my experience with funeral homes, the process has always seemed too standardized with few options. You have very little time to think before making decisions regarding the arrangements. Here are some areas that the decision maker has to consider when finalizing the funeral arrangements.

The Choices

For most of us, the choices are either to have a funeral service or not, which typically requires embalming or cremation. I have only heard of a few Black people who have family members or friends that were cremated. Most of our funerals include embalming, expensive sealed caskets, and burial vaults. While these items are not mandated by law, traditional memorial parks may require them. Most Black funerals are held six to seven days after a person dies. I always thought there was some real reason for the time delay. However, this time is really spent coordinating the arrangements and allowing for out of town family members to travel to the funeral. Obviously, this requires significant money and resources and puts a strain on many families. When the costs required to travel to and from the funeral are too great or family members cannot afford to take time off from work, some loved ones simply have to stay home and miss the funeral.

The Coffin—Which Model?

The choice about the coffin is perhaps the most emotional part of the funeral process. You are made to feel that if Big Momma doesn't lie in the finest, most elaborate coffin, you are lower than the space underneath the belly of a pregnant ant. Each time I went through the coffin selection process, I had this feeling. Since I was the one making the decision for a couple of our recent funerals, I had to remind myself that at the end of the day, no matter which coffin I selected, it was going into the ground and hopefully never to be used or seen again. Do I really want to spend a lot of money for something that will be put into the ground and covered with dirt?

In the movie *The Big Lebowski*, there is a scene where Jeff Bridges and John Goodman are at a funeral chapel discussing burial arrangements for their friend. At this stage in their lives, they are looking for the most meager urn to hold their friend's remains. After a heated discussion with the funeral representative regarding costs, the two men are shown standing on a hill looking over the Pacific ocean with the ashes of their friend in a Folgers coffee can—the most meager urn available was still too costly.[3]

While the cost of funerals is certainly a concern for many families, only recently have many people like myself begun to consider the impact the typical funeral and burial have on the environment. Following are some statistics compiled by the Pre-Posthumous Society of Ithaca, New York.

Each year in the United States, we bury:
- 827,060 gallons of embalming fluid, which includes formaldehyde
- 180,544,000 pounds of steel (in caskets)
- 5,400,000 pounds of copper and bronze (in caskets)
- 30 million board feet of hardwoods, including tropical woods (in caskets)
- 3,272,000,000 pounds of reinforced concrete (in vaults)
- 28,000,000 pounds of steel (in vaults)[4]

As a result of high funeral costs and high impact to our environment, green burials are becoming more popular.

What Is a Green Burial?

A green burial is simple, natural and ensures the burial site remains as natural as possible in all respects. Interment of the bodies is done in a biodegradable casket, shroud, or a favorite blanket. No embalming fluid, no concrete vaults.[5]

In keeping with your personal values, a natural burial site for you, your family, and even your pets promotes the growth of native trees, shrubs, and wildflowers, in turn bringing birds and other wildlife to the area. Water is not wasted; pesticides and herbicides are not used in attempts to control nature. Instead, a green cemetery allows nature to take its course. Planting native trees, shrubs, and flowers in your loved one's honor promotes habitat restoration. To encourage land preservation, a green cemetery grants a conservation easement for the burial site. Some natural or green cemeteries allow, but do not require, stone markers as long as they are of stone native to the area and are employed in a way to enhance ecological restoration.

Until recently, interment in an environmentally friendly burial ground was not an option. Now, families can consider a natural burial, helping to preserve open spaces throughout the United States.

Choosing a green burial and planning for it now relieves your loved ones of the distress that comes in having to make difficult, and often costly, decisions after your passing. Involve your friends and family now, so difficult decisions do not need to be made in a time of grief.[6]

Green Burial Costs

National Public Radio's *All Things Considered* produced a segment on green burials featuring the Ramsey Creek Preserve. The cost of a green burial starts around $2,000, which includes the burial site. A pine casket can cost $420, a cardboard casket as little as $50. As I stated earlier, the cost of a traditional funeral can range from $3,000 to $10,000 when including cemetery costs such as a lot, vault, and plot marker. Many funerals run well over $10,000.[7]

As for me—bury me green.

Chapter 9
The Future of Green

Throughout this book, I have made the case for why Black people should embrace the green movement, and I have provided ways to achieve this. Since starting this project, many of my friends, family members, and colleagues have taken steps toward going green. Almost every day, information is provided on television, in newspapers, on the radio, and in magazines about going green. The individual strides we make are great and necessary; however, if we are going to make huge gains in saving the environment, the future must include broad scale legislation that includes incentives to large manufacturers—especially automobile manufacturers—green job training and, of course, significant reduction of greenhouse gas emissions.

Legislating Green

The city of Chicago has announced one of the most aggressive plans to reduce greenhouse gases. This will further position Chicago among the most environmentally friendly cities in the nation.[1] The Chicago Climate Action Plan outlines a road map of 29 actions that might be taken to reduce greenhouse gas in four areas: buildings; transportation; energy; and waste pollution. The plan also identifies nine actions that could help the city adapt to the changes already occurring. Because the Chicago Climate Action Plan takes a long-term approach, it will be evaluated over time to determine where these actions should be modified or revised. This flexible approach allows for the accommodation of new technologies, new laws, and new opportunities as they evolve. Chicago is already working to implement three of the ideas included in the plan:

1. A "Green Office Challenge" that will spur high-rise office buildings to save energy, to increase recycling and water efficiency, and to reduce paper.

2. An updated Chicago Energy Efficiency Building Code, which will bring the current code up to international standards and make it easier to understand.
3. Innovative ways to help property owners save money by making their buildings more energy efficient.

Other steps proposed in the plan Chicago is considering include large-scale solar energy installations at city facilities; new partnerships to make it easier for residents and businesses to take greater advantage of public transportation; and the construction of four publicly accessible alternative fueling stations.[2]

Yes We Can

At the time of this writing, we have just elected the first Black president in the history of the United States. In a landslide victory, Barack Obama's messages of "Change We Can Believe In" and "Yes We Can" transcended racial lines. As the world watched the amazing victory celebration in Grant Park in Chicago that historic night, some friends invited our family over to watch the election returns; and we all took our children to the gathering to join in the excitement. We wanted to make sure they experienced history in the making so that years from now they can say, "I was there."

As we celebrated that night, I kept thinking about the enormous challenges Barack Obama will face. These challenges include a global economy in shambles, the infrastructure in the United States that is in dire need of repair, a health care system with approximately 45 million uninsured Americans,[3] and the need to establish a real environmental policy to cut greenhouse gas emissions and put America on the path toward mass scale renewable, sustainable energy alternatives. I read the "Obama-Biden New Energy for America Plan" and was very impressed on how comprehensive it is. Here are some key areas worth noting:

Barack Obama and Joe Biden: New Energy for America

Implement Cap-and-Trade Program to Reduce Greenhouse Gas Emissions. Barack Obama and Joe Biden support implementation of an economy-wide cap-and-trade system to reduce carbon emissions by the amount scientists say is necessary: 80 percent below 1990 levels by 2050. This market mechanism has worked before and will give all American consumers and businesses the incentives to use their ingenuity to develop economically effective solutions to climate change. The Obama-Biden cap-and-trade policy will require all pollution credits to be auctioned. A 100 percent auction ensures that all industries pay for every ton of emissions they release, rather than giving these valuable emission rights away to companies on the basis of their past pollution. A small portion of the receipts generated by auctioning allowances

($15 billion per year) will be used to support the development of clean energy, invest in energy efficiency improvements, and help develop the next generation of biofuels and clean energy vehicles—measures that will help the economy and help meet the emissions reduction targets. It will also be used to provide new funding to state and federal land and wildlife managers to restore habitat, create wildlife migration corridors, and assist fish and wildlife to adapt to the effects of a warming climate. All remaining receipts will be used for rebates and other transition relief to ensure that families and communities are not adversely impacted by the transition to a new energy, low carbon economy.

Make the U.S. a Leader on Climate Change. Both Barack Obama and Joe Biden understand that the only real solution to climate change requires all major emitting nations to join in the solution. While it is time for America to lead, developing nations like China and Brazil must not be far behind in making their own binding commitments. To develop an effective and equitable global program, Barack Obama and Joe Biden will re-engage with the U.N. Framework Convention on Climate Change (UNFCC)—the main international forum dedicated to addressing the climate problem. They will also invigorate the Major Economies Meeting (MEM) effort and bring all the major emitting nations together to develop effective emissions reduction efforts.

Create New Job Training Programs for Clean Technologies. The Obama-Biden plan will increase funding for federal workforce training programs and direct these programs to incorporate green technologies training, such as advanced manufacturing and weatherization training, into their efforts to help Americans find and retain stable, high-paying jobs. Barack Obama and Joe Biden will also create an energy-focused youth jobs program to invest in disconnected and disadvantaged youth. This program will provide youth participants with energy efficiency and environmental service opportunities to improve the energy efficiency of homes and buildings in their communities, while also providing them with practical skills and experience in important career fields of expected high-growth employment. Participants will not only be able to use their training to find new jobs, but also build skills that will help them move up the career ladder over time.

Build More Livable and Sustainable Communities. Over the long term, we know that the amount of fuel we will use is directly related to our land use decisions and development patterns. For the last 100 years, our communities have been organized around the principle of cheap gasoline. Barack Obama and Joe Biden believe that we must devote substantial resources to repairing our roads and bridges. They also believe that we must devote significantly more attention to investments that will make it easier for us to walk, bicycle and access other transportation alternatives. They are committed to reforming the federal transportation funding and leveling employer incentives for driving and public transit.[4]

Barack Obama's election undoubtedly has worldwide implications. He has the vision, the charisma, and the determination to really do something positive and profound with the mandate he has been given. As he said throughout the campaign, the green economy will play a major role in pulling us out of the economic crisis. There has never been a greater opportunity than now to bring a vision to Pennsylvania Avenue to help save the environment. If anyone can put us on that path to sustainability, it is Barack Obama. He defied all the odds by winning the election, and in so doing, he created a movement that is eager to demonstrate "yes we can"!

At the beginning of this book, I indicated that the issues of greenhouse gas emissions and climate change were not enough to mobilize the greater Black community to go green at this time. I made this statement well over a year before the democratic primaries began, which ultimately led to Barack Obama's election night win. President Obama will heighten the awareness around these issues and in so doing, the Black community must at least become engaged in the discussion. While we may not be immediately concerned about the adverse impact the melting Arctic ice cap has on the survivability of polar bears, we are, nevertheless, affected by extreme weather conditions that are a result of a warmer planet.

As Blacks, we are proud that Barack Obama won the election. As a community we should pledge our help to him, which means we help ourselves. Many of the areas I've covered in this book are where we can begin to get involved. While President Obama will undoubtedly tackle the bigger climate change and greenhouse gas emissions problems, let us now look at the future of green from a more practical, neighborhood perspective.

Eco Homes

I did not have to travel far to get a glimpse of the future of the green home. *Smart Home: Green + Wired®*," which opened in May 2008, is located on the grounds of the Museum of Science and Industry, not far from where I live in Chicago. Michelle Kaufman was the architect of *Smart Home: Green + Wired®* and built the three-bedroom house on five eco–friendly principles she originated:

1. Smart Design—built to "let the green in." High ceilings, warm materials, clean lines and abundant light and breezes make the home feel even more spacious. A fully automated smart technology system enables homeowners to control heat, window coverings, lighting, security sensors and cameras, as well as track electricity, gas and water consumption in real-time.

2. Material Efficiency—*Smart Home: Green + Wired®* was prefabricated, built in modules off-site. Crafted in a controlled indoor environment, the construction timeline was shortened. Because it was built in this controlled environment, less energy and fewer resources were used than would be required to build a traditional home. Materials used in the construction are renewable or recycled: bamboo flooring, FSC-certified wood and recycled glass tiles are a few of the low-impact choices.
3. Energy Efficiency—High tech. Low impact. Throughout the home, materials and technology help save energy. The green-roof garden helps cool in the summer, insulate during winter months, and absorbs precipitation reducing water runoff. Huge windows, sliding doors and sunshades help light, heat and cool the house. Solar rooftop panels generate much of the home's electricity. Energy Star appliances and an array of energy-efficiency technologies help as well.
4. Water Efficiency –Water is the earth's most precious resource, yet in traditional homes, more than one-quarter of drinking-quality water is used to flush toilets. The Smart Home features an array of energy-efficient technologies and appliances such as low-flow showerheads and dual-flush toilets that generally use less than a gallon of water each time. Rainwater and grey water (water from the shower, tub, washing machine, etc.) are used to not only flush the toilets but also to replenish outdoor greenery.
5. Healthy Environment—In building the Smart Home, non-toxic materials were used: these included no or low-VOC paints; air filtration and purification systems; and spray-in foam insulation, which is more effective than fiberglass batting and minimizes mold. A healthy environment continues outside the home with water recycling systems to hydrate plants, native plants that are better adapted to climate conditions, permeable paving materials and more.[5]

I took the tour of *Smart Home: Green + Wired®* as soon as it opened. The tour usually includes about 10-15 people and is conducted by a tour guide who explains the various green features throughout the home. My wife took our children a few weeks later. During their tour, my son would yell out in excitement when he encountered different things in the house he was familiar with. He was quick to point out the dual-flush toilet, the countertop compost canister, the tankless water heater and the hybrid vehicle in the garage. Obviously, the adults in the group were impressed, and one lady pulled my wife to the side and asked if my son attended a popular private school in the area. My wife smiled, told the woman that our son attends a really good public school that does teach them about the importance of saving the environment, but that he really learned these things at home.

While I illustrate why Black people should embrace the green movement, I try to practice what I preach. We own a hybrid, we have installed CFLs throughout the house, we installed a tankless water heater, we compost appropriate food and yard waste in the backyard, and we wash clothes in cold water, among many other things. Perhaps the most significant green thing we do is explain to our children why we make these purchases, and why we institute certain practices like washing clothes in cold water, and how these products and practices help save money and the environment. The hope is that the lessons they learn as children will remain with them throughout their lives.

As impressive as the *Smart Home: Green + Wired*® is, it too will be improved upon in the future to be even more eco-friendly and efficient. In many cities across the country, there are similar homes, although few in number. Hopefully, in the near future we will see more cities and towns that have been built entirely green.

Meet Greensburg, Kansas

Greensburg, Kansas, is a town that was devastated by a tornado in May 2007 and city officials decided to rebuild—green. I was impressed by a CBS Morning News *special broadcast from Greensburg, and decided that visiting this town would not only be a learning experience for me, but it would also allow me to touch and feel what I hope to be the future of green.*

Not knowing a single person in Greensburg, Kansas, I called the Chamber of Commerce to inquire about the town and was given a few contacts. After some more phone calls, the trip was confirmed. I flew into Wichita and made the two-hour drive to Greensburg. Upon arrival I met Daniel Wallach, director of Greensburg-Greentown, a nonprofit organization established to provide the residents of Greensburg with the resources, information, and support they need to rebuild Greensburg as a model green community in the wake of the May 2007 tornado.

Prior to the tornado, Greensburg was a town with a population of 1400 residents. The people worked in various capacities in the oil industry and farming. With the majority of the town and businesses destroyed, the mayor, Daniel Wallach, and a few others saw an opportunity to rebuild Greensburg in a way that would be environmentally friendly.

Many of the buildings are being built LEED certified. One can't help but notice the art museum, which is being built by students from Kansas State University. The town is busy with construction and people trying to get their lives back to some degree of normalcy. Yet, they take time out to share their experience and success with constant visitors like me, who want to get firsthand information on how to adopt Greensburg's model in their own towns and cities. When asked how officials were able to convince the majority of the city to adopt the go green plan, Wallach described the process as a calculated approach. The organizers of Greensburg-Greentown listened a lot and tried as much as possible to defuse political issues. "We framed the discussion in a way residents could relate."[6]

A key to the success of Greensburg-Greentown was the tornado itself. As almost every home was destroyed and had to be rebuilt anyway, the thinking was, why not rebuild in a way that saves energy, saves money, is environmentally friendly and helps to keep local families intact by creating jobs. I constantly reflect on my trip to Greensburg, Kansas. The planning and development that were done to make Greensburg a reality must be among the models for future green cities. When a tragedy of nature occurs, such as the tornado that struck Greensburg, and the opportunity to rebuild an entire city or town presents itself, then policies and principles rooted in green design must be standard. Every time I reflect on Greensburg, I think about the feeling I had on the plane ride back home to Chicago. My real wish was that I was returning from New Orleans.

End Notes

Chapter 1: Going Green Starts at Home
1. U.S. Bureau of Transportation Statistics, 2007.
2. *The Green Guide,* Spring 2008, pg. 61.
3. Wikipedia, www.wikipedia.org, January 21, 2007.
4. Philippe Bourseiller, *365 Ways to Save the Earth*, Abrams, 2005.
5. "Freshen Up Your Drink," *Time Magazine*, March 24, 2008, page 65.
6. "Cracking the Code: Picking the Best Plastics for Storing Your Food and Drink," *The Green Guide*, Spring 2008, pg. 48.
7. Philippe Bourseiller, *365 Ways to Save the Earth*, Abrams, 2005.
8. Mariette Mifflin, "Your Guide to Housewares / Appliances," about.com Website. Viewed November 23, 2007.
9. "Run the dishwasher only when full," *The Green Guide*, Spring 2008, page 66.
10. Charlene Dy, "How To Stop Being a Drip," *Newsweek*, August 3, 2007, page 57.
11. Philippe Bourseiller, *365 Ways to Save the Earth*, Abrams, 2005.
12. "Don't linger in the shower," *The Green Guide*, Spring 2008, page 74.
13. Ben Lieberman, "Low-flow revolt, Congress looks at repealing new toilet standard," August 8, 1998.
14. Emily Main, "The Economical Bedroom," thegreenguide.com, August 6, 2007.
15. Frank Clark, *Muhammad and Friends*, Cable Access Television, July 15, 2007.
16. Energy Star, www.energystar.gov Website. Viewed July January 13, 2007.
17. Peoples Gas Website, www.peoplesenergy.com, November 23, 2007
18. Francine Knowles, "No-car days, ComEd pricing plan help save money." *Chicago Sun Times,* July 11, 2008.
19. Philippe Bourseiller, *365 Ways to Save the Earth*, Abrams, 2005.
20. "What is Composting," www.Wisegeek.com, August 15, 2007.
21. Ibid.
22. "About Wangari Maathai," www.Greenbeltmovement.org, November 11, 2008.

Chapter 2: Rediscovering Your Neighborhood
1. Personal interview with Rosalind Ali, August 2, 2007.
2. American Community Garden Assoc., www.CommunityGarden.org Website. Viewed July 1, 2007.
3. Ibid.
4. Sustainable South Bronx, www.ssbx.org Website. Viewed August 12, 2008.

Chapter 3: Food and Its Environmental Impact
1. American Heart Association, "Heart Facts 2005: All Americans /African Americans," www.AmericanHeart.org Website. Viewed July 10, 2005.
2. California Dietary Practices Survey: 2003, "Cancer Prevention and Nutrition" Section, California Department of Health Services
3. Food Deserts, www.fooddeserts.org Website. Viewed September 15, 2008.
4. Michelle Bery, "Organic Baby Food—A Healthy Choice," EzineArticles.com Website: Viewed August 23, 2007.
5. Ibid

6. "Rebalance your plate," *The Green Guide*, Spring 2008, page 74.
7. Ibid.
8. Ibid.
9. Don Terry, "Green Acres: A new crop of ecology-friendly farmers say goodbye to city life," *Chicago Tribune Magazine*, July 15, 2007, page 12.
10. "Eat in," *The Green Guide*, Spring 2006, page 73.
11. Philippe Bourseiller, *365 Ways to Save the Earth*, Abrams, 2005
12. Ibid.
13. 2008 MRI Doublebase.
14. Michael Specter, "In measuring carbon emissions, it's easy to confuse morality and science," *The New Yorker* magazine, February 25, 2008
15. Ibid.

Chapter 4: The Electric Car Is Here
1. The Emissions of Greenhouse Gases: Department of Energy Annual Report, November 2007.
2. Goloco.org Website, The Ride Revolution. Viewed December 6, 2007.
3. Ibid.
4. "China Begins Car-Rationing in Beijing Leading up to the Olympics," Ecowordly.com, November 2, 2008.
5. Lester R. Brown, *Plan B 2.0: Rescuing a Planet Under Stress and a Civilization in Trouble,* W.W. Norton & Co., 2006.
6. Todd Kaho, "Green Your Car", *Green Guide Magazine*, Spring 2008, page 35.
7. www.zipcars.com Website. Viewed September 12, 2007.
8. "Bike and Ride," *Guide to Chicago*, June 2008.
9. "Toyota Hybrid System," Toyota Owner's Manual 2007. Reprinted with permission.
10. Shirley Henderson, "Black and Green: The New Eco Warriors," *Ebony Magazine*, July 2008, page 98.
11. *Who Killed the Electric Car?* Chris Paine, Director. Sony Pictures Classics 2006.
12. Ibid.
13. Ibid.
14. Ibid.
15. Ibid.
16. Bill Moore, "Color Me Green," EV World.Com, Inc., Bill Moore Publisher. Reprinted with permission.
17. Daniel Roth, "Driven," *Wired Magazine*, September 2008, page 118.
18. *Who Killed the Electric Car?* Chris Paine, Director. Sony Pictures Classics, 2006.

Chapter 5: Invoking Green in Education
1. Black Alliance for Educational options / Center for Civic Innovation Report, 2007.
2. *Super Size Me*, Morgan Spurlock, Director. Samuel Goldwyn Films/Roadside Attractions 2004.
3. National Black Farmers Association, www.blackfarmers.org Website. Viewed August 26, 2007.

4. Department of Education, www.ed.gov Website, List of HBCUs—White House Initiative on Historically Black Colleges and Universities. Viewed April 8, 2007.
5. "Morrill Land Grant Colleges Act," www.wikipedia.com. Viewed April 9, 2007.
6. University of Maryland Eastern Shore, www.umes.edu, "1890 Land Grant History." Viewed 1/15/09.
7. "Morrill Land Grant Colleges Act," www.wikipedia.com. Viewed April 9, 2007.
8. "George Washington Carver," www.wikipedia.com Website. Viewed May 30, 2007.
9. Tuskegee University, www.tuskegee.edu website. Viewed July 3, 2008.
10. Anne Underwood, "The Green Campus," *Newsweek*, August 20, 2007, page 60.
11. Ibid.
12. Personal interview with Arthur E. Frazier III, AIA Director, Facilities Management & Services, Spelman College, October 2, 2008.
13. Connecticut College, www.conncoll.edu Website. Viewed August 27, 2007.

Chapter 6: Cashing In on Green

1. Personal interview with Daniel Wallach, Director, Greensburg-Greentown. August 12, 2008.
2. "Renewable Energy and Energy Efficiency- Economic Drivers for the 21st Century." Used with permission from the American Solar Energy Society (ASES). All rights reserved.
3. Ibid.
4. Ibid.
5. Lester R. Brown, *Plan B 2.0: Rescuing a Planet Under Stress and a Civilization in Trouble,* W.W. Norton & Co., 2006.
6. Ibid.
7. "Biography of Van Jones." Reprinted with permission from Mr. Van Jones, 2008.
8. "Socially Responsible Investing," www.wikipedia.com Website. Viewed May 18, 2007.
9. As reported in the 2007 Report on Socially Responsible Investing Trends in the United States, Social Investment Forum.
10. "What is Advocacy Investing?" Marc J. Lane Investment Management, Inc., 2008. Reprinted with permission.

Chapter 7: Black Institutions That Should Be Green

1. CNN Website, "Detroit is nation's fattest city," January 2, 2004. Viewed April 15, 2007.
2. America's Fattest and Fittest Cities 2005, *Men's Fitness* magazine.
3. Illinois State Treasurer Report: "Green Rewards-buy green, save green," February 2, 2008.
4. Urban Mobility Report. "Annual Delay Per Traveler, 1982–2005."
5. American Lung Association Website. Viewed February 14, 2008.
6. Atlanta BeltLine, Inc. 2008 website. Viewed July 28, 2008.
7. Charlene Muhammad, "U.S. Blacks ill-prepared for disasters," *Final Call* newspaper, July 31, 2007.

8. Washington, DC Economic Partnership, wdcep.com Website. Viewed
    November 10, 2007.
9. Ibid.
10. Angela Chang, Haley Shapley and Jana Wallis, "What a Wonderful World,"
    AmericanWay magazine, October 1, 2007, pg. 81.
11. "San Francisco—First city to ban plastic shopping bags," *The San Francisco
    Chronicle*, March 28, 2007.
12. Angela Chang, Haley Shapley and Jana Wallis, "What a Wonderful World,"
    AmericanWay magazine, October 1, 2007, pg. 81.
13. Eco Politics," *Newsweek*, November 19, 2007.
14. Abysinnian.org Website. Viewed April 25, 2007.
15. West Angeles, westa.org Website. Viewed April 25, 2007.
16. The Coalition for the Remembrance of Elijah Muhammad Archives, August 4,
    2007.

Chapter 8: Bury Me Green

1. Cheryl Corley, "Burials and Cemeteries Go Green," National Public Radio,
    December 16, 2007.
2. Funeral Costs, Toney Funeral Home, Birmingham, Alabama, permission to
    reprint, 2008.
3. *The Big Lebowski,* Joel Coen, Director. Gramercy Pictures 1998.
4. "Eco-cemetery," www.wikipedia.org Website. Viewed November 1, 2008.
5. Green Burials, www.greenburials.org Website. Viewed December 25, 2007.
6. Ibid.
7. Cheryl Corley, "Burials and Cemeteries Go Green," National Public Radio,
    December 16, 2007.

Chapter 9: The Future of Green

1. Chicago Climate Action Plan, www.chicagoclimateaction.org Website. Viewed
    October 27, 2008.
2. Ibid.
3. "Income, Poverty, and Health Insurance in the United States: 2007," U.S.
    Census Bureau, www.census.gov.
4. "Barack Obama and Joe Biden New Energy for America Plan,"
    Barackobama.com Website. Viewed October 1, 2008.
5. Museum of Science and Industry: Exhibit Resource Guide featuring Smart
    Home: Green + Wired® 2008.
6. Personal interview with Daniel Wallach, director, Greensburg-Greentown,
    August 12, 2008.

Resource Guide

Chapter 1: Going Green Starts at Home
www.eco-me.com
www.ecos.com
www.seasidenaturals.com
www.seventhgeneration.com
www.shaklee.com
www.ewg.org
www.greenhome.com
ecogeekliving.com
ecover.com
luckyearth.com
greenroofs.com
www.eco-furniture.com
www.eco-timber.com

Chapter 2: Rediscovering Your Neighborhood
www.communitygarden.org
www.ssbx.org

Chapter 3: Food and Its Environmental Impact
www.pps.org
http://www.worldchanging.com/archives/007372.html
http://www.biodynamics.com/csa.html
http://www.localharvest.org/csa/
http://newfarm.org/farmlocator/index.php
http://www.wilson.edu/wilson/asp/content.asp?id=1567
http://www.eatwellguide.org/
http://attra.ncat.org/attra-pub/localfood_dir.php

Chapter 4: The Electric Car Is Here
www.zipcar.com
www.goloco.org
www.clean-and-green-cars.blogspot.com
www.chryslerllc.com
www.gm.com/hybrid
www.fordvehicles.com/hybrid
www.toyota.com/prius-hybrid
www.bicyclecity.com

Chapter 5: Invoking Green in Education
www.blackfarmers.org
http://bfaa-us.org
www.buildgreenschools.org
www.greenschools.net
www.kidsforsavingearth.org
www.usgbc.org
www.greenschoolsalliance.org
www.planetgreen.com
www.healthy-kids-go-green.com
www.kids-going-green.com
www.ecochildsplay.com
www.goinggreeny.com

Chapter 6: Cashing In on Green
www.sustainablebusiness.com/jobs
www.greenjobs.com
jobs.greenbiz.com
www.greenjobs.net
www.ecobusinesslinks.com/environmental_jobs.htm
www.greenforall.org

Chapter 7: Black Institutions That Should Be Green
www.churchesgogreen.org
www.nccecojustice.org/grbuilding.htm
www.csmonitor.com
www.blackfarmers.org
www.bfaa-us.org
www.westa.org
abysinnian.org
www.ready.gov/america/makeplan

Chapter 8: Bury Me Green
www.thegreenfuneralsite.com
www.greenburials.org
www.greenburialcouncil.org
www.memorialecosystems.com

Chapter 9: The Future of Green
www.chicagoclimateaction.org
www.msichicago.org
www.greensburggreentown.org

General Information

begreennow.com
plentymag.com
wecansolveit.org
eartheasy.com
thegreenguide.com
environment.about.com
greenpeace.org
conservation.org
greenlivingtips.com
ucsusa.org
www.myfootprint.org
www.greenhotels.com
www.ourearth.org
www.earthpolicy.org

Index

Abyssinian Baptist Church (NYC), 43
Abyssinian Development Corporation
    (ADC), 43
Advocacy Investing strategy, 36
Agassi, Shai, 25
air conditioning, 6
air quality, 21
Alabama Small Farm Rural Economic
    Development Center, 31
algae blooms and phosphates, 3
All Things Considered, 50
alternative fuels, 29–30
American Community Garden
    Association, 12–13
American Lung Association, 38
American Solar Energy Society
    (ASES), 33
antibiotics in animals, 18
appliances, Energy Star®, 3, 55
architects, environmental, 35
Atlanta (GA), 38–39
automobile emissions, 38–39
automobile manufacturers, 38
automobiles. *See also* cars

baby food, organic, 18
"Bag, Borrow or Steal" stores, 5
banquets, 46
bathroom water use, 3–4
battery use in hybrid cars, 23
Beijing and cars, 21–22
The BeltLine green space, 39
bicycles, 22–23; manufacture and
    service, 34
The Big Lebowski, 48–49
biofuel exploration, 29–30
Black and Navy, xiii
Black churches, 42–44
Black cities, 37–40
Black colleges, 28–29
Black Farmer Initiative, 28
Black farmers, 29–30
Black institutions, xvii, 37
Black voters, 41–42
Blake, Charles E., 44

Bloomberg, Michael, 43
Borax, 2
Bridges, Jeff, 48–49
Brown, Lester, 21–22, 34
budget billing plans for utilities, 5–6
building codes, 52
buildings: abandoned, 11; and
    greenhouse gases, 51
burial, xvii, 47–50; environmental
    impact of, 49; green, 49–50
buses, hybrid, 41
Butts, Calvin, 43

California Air Resources Board
    (CARB), 24
Cap-and-Trade Program, 52–53
carbon dioxide emissions, 21, 38–39,
    41
carbon neutrality, 42
cardiovascular disease (CVD), 17
car makers, 38
car pooling, 22
cars: cost of owning, 21; electric, xvii;
    hybrid, xvii, 23–24; restrictions in
    China, 22
Carter, Majora, 14
Carver, George Washington, 30–31
cashing in on green, xvii
cemetery, green, 49
"Change We Can Believe In," 52
chemicals: in cleaning products, 1–2; in
    food, 17–18
Chicago, 41
Chicago Climate Action Plan, 51
Chicago Energy Efficiency Building
    Code, 52
Chicago Tribune Magazine, 19
children, involving, 56
cities, Black, 37–40
"Clean Energy Jobs Corps," 35
cleaning products, 1–2
Clean Technology, Job Training
    Programs for, 53
climate change, 53
climate protection, 41

clothing: overabundance of, 5;
    secondhand, 5
coffins, 48–49
Cole-Kweli, Johari, 19
College of Agricultural,
    Environmental, and Natural
    Sciences (CAENS), 31
Commonwealth Edison, 5, 7
community gardens, 11–14
compact fluorescent light (CFLs), xvi,
    6, 27, 31
composting, 3, 7–8; in schools, 27
Congress, greening, 42
Connecticut College, 31–32
cooking and energy use, 2–3
cotton cultivation, 30
cremation, 48
crime in the community, 14
crops, alternatives to cotton, 30

Democratic Party, 41–42
detergents in cold water, 4–5
Detroit, 37–38
District of Columbia, 40–41
Divine, Colette, 24–25

early adopters, 30
eating in/out, costs compared, 19
eco homes, 54–56
economy, green, 54
education, 27; invoking green in, xvii
electric car EV1, 24–25
electric cars, 21–25; recharge stations,
    25
electricity, saving on, 6
Electric Recharge Grid Operator
    (ERGO), 25
emissions, automobile, 38–39
emotional connection to cars, 23
energy: efficiency, 55; and greenhouse
    gases, 51; renewable, 34; saving
    on, 3
energy-saving tips, 6–7
Energy Star® appliances, 3, 55
environment, saving the, xiv
Environmental Protection Agency
    (EPA), 3
environment and food choices, 18
ethical investing, 35–36
EV1 (electric car), 24–25

family reunions, 45–46
farmers' markets, 20
farming community, 19, 45
farms, black-owned, 28
"Fattest Cities in America," 38
Fenty, Mayor, 41
Final Call, 40
fish, farm-raised, 19–20, 34
fluorescent light bulbs, compact
    (CFLs), xvi, 6, 27, 31
food, xv–xvi; choices, 18; and
    environment, xvi–xvii, 17–20;
    organic, 17–18, 27; transportation
    costs, 20
"food deserts," xvi, 17, 19
food miles and transportation costs, 20
fueling stations, alternative, 52
fuel monitor, 22
fuels, alternative, 29–30
funerals, xvii, 47–50
future of green, xviii, 51–57

garbage composting, 7–8
gardens, community, 11–14; for
    children, 13; committee for, 12;
    communication system for, 13–14;
    organizing plots, 13;
    preparation/development of, 13;
    resources needed, 12; rules in
    writing, 13; site for, 13; sponsor
    for, 13
gardens, rooftop, 41
gas mileage, improvement of, 22
General Motors electric car, 24–25
"Genius" Grant, 14
Go Green directory, 4
Goodman, John, 48–49
Gore, Al, xiii
grass clippings, 7–8
Green Belt Movement, 9
Green Building Rating System, 31
green cities, notable, 40–41
Green-Collar Jobs Advisory Council,
    40–41
Green-Collar Jobs report, 33–34
Green Cup (Harvard), 31
Green for All, 35
Green Guide magazine, 19
green home, 54–56

greenhouse gas emissions, 21, 38–39, 41, 51, 52
green is cool, 30
green jobs, 33–35
Green Jobs Act of 2007, 35
"Green Jobs Corps," 35
"Green Office Challenge," 51
Greensburg-Greentown (KS), 57
Greensburg (KS), xviii, 57
green space, urban, 39
green starts at home, xvi
"Green the ghetto!", 14
grey water use, 55
grocery stores, 17
growth hormones in animals, 18

Harvard University, 31
health of the Black community, 17
Historically Black Colleges and Universities (HBCUs), 28–29
homeless people and jobs, 15
home-office jobs, 34
homes: design for energy efficiency, 54; eco, 54–56; and going green, 1–8
hormones, growth, 18
"Hotlanta," 38
Hunts Point Riverside Park, 14
Hurricane Katrina, 39–40
hybrid cars, 23–24; incentives to buy, 38

An Inconvenient Truth, xiii
industries, energy efficiency, 34
interment, 48–49
investing, green, 35–36
irrigation technology, 34

Jackson, Jesse Jr., 43
Jackson, Sandy, 43
jobs: creation of, 33–35; for the homeless, 15
Job Training Programs for Clean Technology, 53
Jones, Van, 35
Jubilee 2000 Africa Campaign, 9

Kaufman, Michelle, 54
key influencers, 30
kitchen, 2

kitchen garbage in composting, 7–8
Kyoto climate treaty, 41

Land-Grant College Act, 29
land-grant HBCUs, 29
laundry, xvi; and phosphate levels, 3
Leadership in Energy and Environmental Design (LEED), 31, 57
leased electric cars, 24–25
legislation, green, 51–54
light bulbs, xvi, 6, 27, 31
linens, bed, 4
liquid crystal display (LCD) as energy saver, 3
local food sources, 20
Lurie, Neal, 33

Maathai, Wangari, 9
MacArthur "Genius" Grant, 14
Major Economies Meeting (MEM), 53
"make do," xv
Malcolm X, 37
Marc J. Lane Investment Management, Inc., 36
Marine Stewardship Council, 19
markets, farmers', 20
material efficiency, 55
mattresses, organic materials, 4
meat, resources required for, 18
Meeks, James, 43
Men's Fitness Magazine, 38
metric shift, xiii–xiv
Metropolitan Atlanta Rapid Transit Authority (MARTA), 39
modular home design, 55
moral imperative, xiv
Morrill, Justin, 29
Morrill Acts of 1862 and 1890, 28
Mount Trashmore, 31
Muhammad, Elijah, 45
Museum of Science and Industry (Chicago), 54

National Public Radio, 50
neighborhood, xvi, 14–15; black, 37; rediscovering your, 11–15
neighborhood, blighted, 11
New Energy for America, 52–53
New Orleans, 39–40

Nobel Peace Prize (2004) to Wangari
    Maathai, 9
non-toxic materials, 55

Obama, Barack, 52–54
"Obama-Biden New Energy for
    America Plan," 52–53
office buildings, 51
Olympics (2008), 21
Operation Trim the Fat, 38
organic farming, 19
Ozone-Polluted Cities, 25 Most, 39

packaging, food, 27
Pan-African Green Belt Network, 9
peanut industry, 30
Pelosi, Nancy, 42
Pembroke (IL) farming community, 19
pesticides, 4, 7; in food, 17–18
phosphates and algae blooms, 3
picnics, 46
pillows, 4
Plan B 2.0: Rescuing a Planet Under
    Stress and a Civilization in
    Trouble, 21–22, 34
plastic bags, banned, 41
political parties, 41–42
pollution, 52
polyethylene terephthalate (PET) in
    water bottles, 2
prefabricated home design, 55
Pre-Posthumous Society, 49
produce, local, 20
Project Better Place, 25
property owners, 52

rail, light, 35
rainwater runoff, 7
Ramsey Creek Preserve, 50
re-charge stations for electric cars, 25
recycling, 46; jobs for homeless, 15; in
    the kitchen, 2–3; numbers/symbols,
    2
reduce, reuse, and recycle, xiv, 46
refrigerators, 7, 31
regenerative brake, 23–24
Republican Party, 41
reuse, xiii–xvi
right turns to save gas, 22
Roots, 45

Salem Baptist Church (Chicago), 43
San Francisco, 41
schools, waste in, 27
science fairs, 28
Seattle, 41
shopping: grocery, 18; locally, 20
Small Farm Center, 31
Smart Home: Green + Wired®, 54–56
soap, use all of it, 4
Socially responsible investing (SRI),
    35–36
sodium borate, 2
solar energy, 52
soul food, xv
Spelman College, 31
spoilage of food, 18
stand-by mode for energy saving, 3
Super Size Me, 27
sustainability, 42, 54
sustainable: communities, 53–54;
    investing, 35–36; living, 32
Sustainable South Bronx (SSB), 14
sweet potatoes, 30

tankless water heater, 55
teach green, 28
technology, green, 54–56
telecommuting, 34
thermostat adjustments, 6
time-of-day: special rates, 6–7
toilets, water-saving, 4
tornado damage, xviii, 57
transportation: alternative methods, 53–
    54; and greenhouse gases, 21, 38–
    39, 51; light rail, 34; public, 22, 52
transportation costs for food, 20
trees, planting, 8, 35
t-shirts for family reunions, 46
Tuskegee Institute, 29

U.N. Framework Convention on
    Climate Change (UNFCC), 53
United Parcel Service (UPS), 22
Urban Mobility Report, 38
U.S. Navy radio commercial, xiii
utilities: budget billing plans, 5–6; and
    energy saving, 6–7

vacant lots, problems, 11
vertical integration in production, 45

vote green, 41–42

walking, 22
walking club, 15
Wallach, Daniel, 33, 57
Washington, Kerry, 24
Washington (DC), 40–41
waste: of food, 18; pollution and
    greenhouse gases, 51; in schools,
    27
water: aerator on faucet, 2;
    conservation of, 2–4; drinking, xiv;
    efficient use of, 55; productivity,
    34
water bottles, plastic, 2

water heater, tankless, 55
West Angeles Church of God in Christ
    (Los Angeles), 44
"What would Jesus do?", 42
Who Killed the Electric Car?, 24
"Why should I care?", xiv–xv
Willams College (MA), 31
"Worst Commutes," 38

yard, in the, 7–8
"Yes We Can," 52
"Your Supermarket," 45

Zero Emissions mandate, 24
Zipcar®, 22